T0328609

Cambridge Elements ≡

Elements in Music Since 1945
edited by
Mervyn Cooke
University of Nottingham

CHINESE ÉMIGRÉ COMPOSERS AND DIVERGENT MODERNISMS

Chen Yi and Zhou Long

Mia Chung
Curtis Institute of Music

CAMBRIDGE
UNIVERSITY PRESS

Shaftesbury Road, Cambridge CB2 8EA, United Kingdom

One Liberty Plaza, 20th Floor, New York, NY 10006, USA

477 Williamstown Road, Port Melbourne, VIC 3207, Australia

314–321, 3rd Floor, Plot 3, Splendor Forum, Jasola District Centre, New Delhi – 110025, India

103 Penang Road, #05–06/07, Visioncrest Commercial, Singapore 238467

Cambridge University Press is part of Cambridge University Press & Assessment, a department of the University of Cambridge.

We share the University's mission to contribute to society through the pursuit of education, learning and research at the highest international levels of excellence.

www.cambridge.org
Information on this title: www.cambridge.org/9781009475761

DOI: 10.1017/9781009158817

First published 2024

A catalogue record for this publication is available from the British Library.

ISBN 978-1-009-47576-1 Hardback
ISBN 978-1-009-15880-0 Paperback
ISSN 2632-7791 (online)
ISSN 2632-7783 (print)

Chinese Émigré Composers and Divergent Modernisms

Chen Yi and Zhou Long

Elements in Music Since 1945

DOI: 10.1017/9781009158817
First published online: April 2024

Mia Chung
Curtis Institute of Music

Author for correspondence: Mia Chung, mia.chungyee@gmail.com

Abstract: This Element examines the factors that drove the stylistic heterogeneity of Chen Yi and Zhou Long after the Cultural Revolution. Known as "New Wave" composers, they entered the Central Conservatory of Music once the Cultural Revolution ended and attained international recognition for their modernisms after their early careers in America. Scholars have often treated their early music as contingent outcomes of that cultural and political moment. This Element proposes instead that unique personal factors shaped their modernisms despite their shared experiences of the Cultural Revolution and educations at the Central Conservatory and Columbia University. Through interviews on six stages of their development, the Element examines and explains the reasons for their stylistic divergence.

This Element also has a video abstract: www.cambridge.org/EM45_Chung

Keywords: Cultural Revolution, musical modernism, Zhou Long, Chen Yi, New Wave composers

ISBNs: 9781009475761 (HB), 9781009158800 (PB), 9781009158817 (OC)
ISSNs: 2632-7791 (online), 2632-7783 (print)

Contents

1 Introduction

The Cultural Revolution ended in September 1976, leaving a traumatized populace. For ten years, Mao purged China of Western and traditional Chinese thought and cultural practice to consolidate his power within the Communist party. After his death, the musical vestiges of this period that promoted his political agenda disappeared, including *yangbanxi*, the government-approved revolutionary musical genre. Gone were the devastating prohibitions enforced by Mao's regime, and in their wake emerged new educational possibilities that facilitated a genuine revolution in Chinese music. By 1978, conservatory doors reopened, and a generation of young composers who had served in the labor camps matriculated, free to study music without the fear of government reprisal. Eventually, several emigrated to the West, becoming the first post-revolutionary modernists, among them Chen Yi (b. April 4, 1953, Guangzhou) and Zhou Long (b. July 8, 1953, Beijing), who were married in 1983.

In twentieth-century China, music was largely a tool for social reform and unifying the masses during major political upheavals. Events such as the Japanese occupation of Manchuria in 1931, the rise of Communism under Mao in 1949, and the Cultural Revolution (1966–76) prevented widespread exposure to Western modernism. The Cultural Revolution's systematic purge of Western influences resulted in the closure of music schools and the prohibition of every type of institutionalized Western musical endeavor, particularly experimentalism. By the time Mao died in 1976, the concept of "art for art's sake" had largely been forgotten in China. Thus, Chen Yi and Zhou Long began their conservatory training when the previous generation's pedagogical influence and pre-Mao Western influences were gradually being rediscovered. As a result, "new styles – individual styles – emerged" that were the combination of "basic techniques learned by New Wave composers from the first and second generations of composers, modern Western composition techniques, and the individual personalities of the New Wave composers" (Liu, 2010, p. 516).[1] It is this final factor that warrants further attention.

Despite their shared experiences as laborers during the Cultural Revolution, students at the Central Conservatory of Music, and advanced degree candidates at Columbia University, Chen and Zhou have distinct personal qualities and narratives that shaped their modernisms. This Element will identify and explore the factors that informed their unique experimentations with Chinese and Western expression most powerfully. Their personalities, family histories,

---

[1] By the 1980s, musicologists began referring to the younger generation of composers emerging after the end of the Cultural Revolution as the "New Wave" or *xin chao* (Liu, 2010, p. 510).

upbringings, and musical experiences at the labor camps, among other factors, emerge as having uniquely shaped the singular forms their modernisms took. Thus, the interplay between personal and external forces before, during, and immediately after the Cultural Revolution suggests a more nuanced understanding than current scholarship offers.

The growing scholarship on Chinese "New Wave" composers largely focuses on cultural identity, the fusion of Eastern and Western compositional philosophies and techniques in their music, or takes the form of analytical discussions of specific works.[2] In contrast to this accepted approach, this Element demonstrates that the development of their modernisms cannot be adequately explained by locating them within the macropolitical or social events of their day but requires an understanding of the contingencies of each composer's life experience and personality. Furthermore, the general description of their music as "East meets West" by critics and scholars alike will emerge as an incomplete characterization of their creative thought processes.

In contrast to the extensive research treating Western composers as distinct products of historical and personal circumstances, comparable understandings of China's "New Wave" composers are nascent and scarce at best.[3] This oversight arises from a popular Western perception that the Cultural Revolution eliminated personal agency, thus preventing "New Wave" works from being treated as uniquely contingent expressions. Hopefully, my examination of Zhou Long's and Chen Yi's family backgrounds, experiences, and formal and informal educations will encourage greater attention to these composers' individuality in future scholarship and promote a more subtle understanding of the genesis and formation of their musical modernisms, particularly in the context of postrevolutionary political change.

The central question this Element explores is: Why are the works of these two composers so stylistically different despite their experiences during and after the Cultural Revolution? Chen and Zhou began diverging artistically as early as their Central Conservatory years and continued doing so once they were in the United States. Notable divergences include Chen Yi's gravitation to the "uptown" essence of Mario Davidovsky, while Zhou Long, influenced by Chou Wen-Chung, adapted the sounds and techniques of ancient Chinese music to the West's modern instruments and ensembles. Since there were unique opportunities Chen and Zhou enjoyed even in the context of political

---

[2] Exceptions to this include *Chen Yi* by Edwards and Miller (2020), which addresses the unique contingencies of the individual and provides a critique of the prevailing East–West cultural synthesis.

[3] This undifferentiated approach applies to Asian composers in general.

repression, this Element considers the personal alongside the external socio-historical forces that shaped their modernist approaches.

This Element begins with an introduction to *yangbanxi*, or government-approved "model works," the single most important musical genre produced during the Cultural Revolution, and a brief history of China's relationship with Western musical culture and pedagogy between 1916 and 1956, when the Shanghai and Central Conservatories of Music were established. This historical macrostructure is followed by a section on the localized influence of Chou Wen-Chung, the "patron saint" of Chinese modernism. Chou played a critical role in bringing these composers to the United States and sharing his aspirations for an "ideal" Chinese modernism, one rooted in traditional Chinese expression yet incorporating Western modernist techniques.

This Element continues with sections devoted to both Zhou Long and Chen Yi that highlight the factors that contributed to their individuality. Early experiences help to explain the divergence of the transcultural modernist styles they later pioneered. The substance of my argument is based on fourteen virtual interviews I conducted with Chen and Zhou in 2021 and 2022. Unless otherwise noted, all quotations and facts are from these interviews.[4]

For greater precision, I define two categories of influence: external and internal. External influences include those that were beyond their control, such as family of origin, childhood learning, and experiences during the Cultural Revolution. Internal influences are unique drivers such as personality, aptitudes, and nature that shaped their music and choices at the Central Conservatory and beyond. The expression of these external and internal factors falls into six defined stages: (1) family history before birth; (2) early childhood (opportunities, exposures, and studies of Western and indigenous Chinese music); (3) labor camp assignments with their experiences and demands (location, nature of the work, rigor and level of government scrutiny); (4) conservatory education after the Cultural Revolution; (5) post-undergraduate work or training; and (6) doctoral studies at Columbia University. I limit my study to experiences and works through 1993, the year Zhou and Chen graduated from Columbia University, because the works from this period are the purest reflections of their modernist proclivities or, as Zhou said, demonstrate what he and Chen were "aiming for." Once commissions began rolling in, their output was informed additionally by the parameters and interests of the commissioner.

The final section synthesizes and compares the major factors that shaped Chen and Zhou's music. I also incorporate statements from virtual interviews

---

[4] These interviews were conducted in English.

with their colleagues, a family member, and friends in 2022 and 2023. The extreme political and social environment of the Cultural Revolution combined with the composers' unique backgrounds and dispositions make it possible to identify the reasons for their stylistic divergence.

2 Musical Context

An exploration of Chen and Zhou's modernisms requires a brief history of the music sanctioned during the Cultural Revolution and the music institutions and pedagogues that played direct and indirect roles in these composers' educations that began in 1978 at the Central Conservatory of Music. A description of *yangbanxi*, which mostly took the form of reformed Beijing operas, is included. A brief survey of conservatory history in China beginning in 1916 follows, concluding with a description of Chou Wen-Chung and his aesthetic philosophy.

2.1 *Yangbanxi*

The Cultural Revolution (1966–76) introduced unprecedented music reforms designed to rid Chinese culture of "Western bourgeois influence" and produce works for public indoctrination. Known as *yangbanxi*, China's "model works" were the only ones performed, replicated, filmed, and screened across the entire country during that era. Among the eight original works were five modernized Beijing operas, two ballets, and one symphony. By the end of the Revolution in 1976, there was a total of nineteen sanctioned works, with eleven being modernized Beijing operas (Dai, 2016, p. 11). A musical fixture for Zhou and Chen in the decade before they entered Beijing's Central Conservatory of Music in 1978, these operas were geared to illiterate peasants, workers, and soldiers and intended to indoctrinate them with Mao Zedong's socialist message. From a musical perspective, however, these works fulfilled a long-standing aspiration to modernize Beijing opera, one that had existed since the turn of the century, long before Mao's ascent. Ironically, the model opera's radical modernization incorporated Western instruments and synthesized Western and Eastern compositional techniques, the contributions of Jiang Qing, Mao's wife, an admirer of Western opera, and Yu Huiyong, the Minister of Culture, an accomplished composer appointed by Jiang.

Beijing opera was a cherished national art form and the beneficiary of a rich tradition. Unlike Western opera, however, traditional Beijing opera was performed collectively by a troupe, with melodies drawn from existing folk tunes. Passed down orally, the operas possessed a formulaic structure, including highly stylized gestures and delivery, symbolism, stock characters, historic costumes, and face masks, and performance conventions such as mime, dance, and martial arts. The music was largely monophonic, with a single improvised or fixed melody carried by a singer or an instrument punctuated with percussion. The opera orchestras were small ensembles of six to eight members, each playing more than one instrument among the four indigenous types: strings, winds, brass, and percussion.

In previous centuries, Beijing opera played an important role of transmitting dynastic values in response to changing social and political climates. During the Qing dynasty (1644–1911), the subject matter was largely romantic, particularly when times were prosperous. In the nineteenth century, however, legendary Chinese emperors, military leaders, and statesmen were represented on stage as reminders of China's illustrious past, an escapist contrast to the reality of British invasion and China's defeat in the Opium Wars (Ludden, 2013, p. 94). The Qing dynasty's last empress, Cixi (1835–1908), brought Beijing opera to a new level, securing its status as the "national opera of China" (Ludden, 2013, p. 53). Her attention to Beijing opera fostered interest among the masses, who identified with the folk stories it portrayed, while legitimizing its development and ongoing refinement among the educated Han (Ludden, 2013, p. 94).

After a relatively continuous development during the Qing dynasty, Beijing opera entered a period of political turbulence and ideological change in the first half of the twentieth century. Calling for Beijing opera's remodeling, Western-educated scholars and artists sought to raise its stature to that of Western opera. The rise of regional opera traditions (North versus South), exposure to Western film and drama, rising tensions between the educated elite and the uneducated masses, and social reforms also encouraged change. Moreover, Beijing opera's epicenter moved from its city of origin to the prosperous, Western-influenced, and intellectually progressive city of Shanghai. The Shanghai School of Beijing opera incorporated modern themes to reflect changing societal norms (departing from Confucian tradition) and spoken drama as inspired by Western dramatic forms.

As one of China's leading art forms during the second half of the twentieth century, Beijing opera became a ready vehicle for educating the masses through storytelling, dance, and music. Mao shared his vision for art at the Yan'an Forum on Literature and Art as early as 1942:

> What we demand, therefore, is a unity of politics and art … a unity of revolutionary political content and the highest artistic form possible … our comrades can definitely transform themselves and their work, creating many fine works that will be enthusiastically welcomed by workers, peasants, and soldiers, and the popular masses. (McDougall, 1980, pp. 76, 78, 86)

This responsibility ultimately fell to Mao's wife, Jiang Qing, who possessed the experience necessary to lead this artistic revolution in Beijing opera, ballet, and orchestral music. As Mao's deputy, Jiang instituted the most comprehensive modernist reforms of Beijing opera and fulfilled Mao's visions for socialist-realist art. The modernized Beijing opera harnessed themes that were accessible to the general public, employed characters such as soldiers, peasants, and workers with whom the masses could identify, had modern-day sets and costumes, adopted standard spoken Mandarin instead of the highly stylized form previously used, and incorporated singing, recited text, performance, and martial arts. The original operas include *Shajiabang*, *The Red Lantern*, *On the Docks*, *Raid on the White Tiger Regiment*, and *Taking Tiger Mountain by Strategy*. Other sanctioned works include two ballets – *The White-Haired Girl* and *The Red Detachment of Women*, and a symphonic work based on *Shajiabang*. More works followed such as the *Yellow River Piano Concerto*. Jiang also extended artistic license to collaborators who upheld Mao's revolutionary values (Ludden, 2013, pp. 202–203). One of these loyalists, Yu Huiyong, made these significant musical reforms possible. The chief architect, composer, orchestrator, and theorist for the *yangbanxi*, Yu became Jiang's right hand in fulfilling the long-standing aspiration for Beijing opera.

Educated during China's Communist era, Yu Huiyong (1925–77) was a respected composer and professor at the Shanghai Conservatory. Well-versed in Chinese indigenous music and the Western tradition, he was both a folk music theorist and a composer capable of revolutionizing Beijing opera (Ludden, 2013, p. 210). Yu transformed Beijing opera by composing the *yangbanxi*, notating the opera scores, amplifying the drama and emotion of the socialist characters, introducing overtures to set the dramatic atmosphere, composing new arias, and abandoning traditional approaches to vocal and instrumental interactions, among other reforms.

Perhaps the most prominent reforms Yu enacted were in the orchestral textures and orchestration. He raised the instrumental content's importance to that of the voice through harmony and counterpoint, while maintaining the voice's audibility. He also included Western instruments in the *yangbanxi* orchestra. Violins, violas, cellos, and other instruments supplemented the Beijing opera orchestra to create sonorities that better conveyed and supported the drama. (Incorporating Western instruments was no small feat for Yu, since Chinese and Western instruments are tuned according to different systems. Also, Western notation was unfamiliar to Chinese instrumentalists.) Yu carefully toed the line between innovation and tradition. His genius was his ability to preserve the look and feel of the Beijing operatic tradition while adapting it for Mao's socialist message. His principal achievement in reforming Beijing opera was using Western instruments and compositional approaches to reach Chinese workers, peasants, and soldiers. Since the dramatic and emotional power resulting from these changes satisfied Jiang's tastes and Communist Party expectations, Yu enjoyed the artistic freedom necessary to reform Beijing opera wholesale. His success in these efforts demonstrated not only his abilities but just how robust Western musical training was prior to the Cultural Revolution.

2.2 Two Major Conservatories

Understanding Chen and Zhou's modernisms calls for an examination of two institutions that played an important role in China's music education during the first half of the century. Through missionaries like the Jesuit Matteo Ricci (1552–1610), China was introduced to Western music as early as the seventeenth century; however, the absorption of Western styles flourished in the twentieth century during the New Culture Movement of the 1910s and 1920s (Everett & Tibbetts, 2018, p. 283). This facilitated the coexistence of Western and Chinese music curricula that spanned most of the twentieth century.

During the May Fourth Movement (1917–21), efforts to organize a music community around Western and Chinese music were in process under the leadership of President Cai Yuanpei at the Peking University. Cai, an educational reformer who had studied in Leipzig and Berlin (Mittler, 1997, p. 25), emphasized education's role in promoting "morality, knowledge, physical exercise, and aesthetics" to create "well-rounded people" (Cai & Melvin, 2004, pp. 93–96).[5] Through an evolving process that spanned several years, "music reform groups" at the Peking University became the Peking University Music Research Group in 1919 and then the Institute for the Promotion and Practice of Music at Peking University in 1921 (Cai & Melvin, 2004, p. 96). Once Xiao Youmei, a musicologist with a PhD from the Leipzig Music Academy joined Cai's efforts, the pedagogical reforms necessary to launch a university-level music program were realized, ones that favored Western music over China's own. An ambitious expansion of classes, performance study, concerts, and other activities ensued. However, after several years of growth, the Northern Warlord government closed the Institute in 1927.

The collaboration of Cai and Xiao continued undeterred. In November 1927, they founded the Shanghai National Music College to provide China's gifted students with a professional-level music education and to complete the work

---

[5] *Rhapsody in Red* by Melvin and Cai serves as a central source for this section unless otherwise noted.

already begun in Peking (Kouwenhoven & Schimmelpenninck, 1993, p. 59). Fashioning the college after the German educational system, Xiao recruited top teaching talent. By 1937, he had hired a number of Russian, European, and Chinese faculty.

Even as the conflict of the Second Sino-Japanese War or "War of Resistance" (1937–45) intensified, Xiao managed to sustain the National Music College. However, a contingent of students and staff from the College moved to Chongqing (Kouwenhoven & Schimmelpenninck, 1993, p. 70), where they established the Qingmuguan College of Music and a separate branch, the Songlinggang College of Music. By the war's end in 1945, the Qingmuguan College of Music relocated to Nanjing, becoming the Nanjing Conservatory of Music, while the Songlinggang College of Music moved to Shanghai (Liu, 2010, p. 93). The Nanjing Conservatory eventually became the Central Conservatory of Music through multiple mergers with schools in Peking. By 1946, a similar merger of the Songlinggang College of Music with the Shanghai National Music College resulted in the Shanghai National Conservatory of Music, so named in 1956.[6] Many of the original Shanghai National Music College graduates went on to teach at these and other conservatories that sprang up across the country, of which the Shanghai and Central Music Conservatories are the largest and most influential.

2.3 Chou Wen-Chung

Once conservatories reopened in 1978, Chou Wen-Chung, the first Chinese composer to achieve recognition in the West, returned to the Central Conservatory of Music to introduce a post–Cultural Revolution generation to Western modernist techniques and the larger philosophical questions regarding cultural synthesis. A composer, educator, and cultural ambassador, Chou was responsible for bringing members of the "New Wave" generation to Columbia University for advanced study and for helping modernism take root in China (Figure 1). In every sense, he was the forerunner and "patron saint" of post-revolutionary modernism, a mantle that Zhou and Chen have taken up admirably for the next generation of Chinese composers. In classmate Tan Dun's words, "[Chou] was the only one who could share a very deep knowledge of the traditions of China, but also bring us into a completely new world. He was the one who built a dream for us" (Da Fonseca-Wollheim, 2019).

---

[6] The history of these conservatories is complicated and made more so by the many name changes and mergers. Only the most significant ones are covered here.

Figure 1 (Left to right) Chen Yi, Chou Wen-Chung, and Zhou Long, 2013
(photo courtesy of Chen Yi)

Born in Yantai in 1923, Chou moved to the United States in 1946 after several years of hardship and displacement due to the Second Sino-Japanese War (1937–45) (Chang, 2006, p. 22). A polymath of sorts, Chou was interested in architecture, engineering, aesthetics, and music. He attended the New England Conservatory of Music, where he studied with Nicholas Slonimsky. Later in New York City, Chou studied with Otto Luening at Columbia University and privately with Edgard Varèse. Chou's contributions as a composer are modest, and yet, he played a pivotal role in developing Chinese modernism by initiating the Center for US-China Arts Exchange in 1978. Once diplomatic relations between the United States and China had normalized in 1979 after a thirty-year hiatus, Chou brought high-profile musicians such as violinist Isaac Stern to China, made teaching trips to the Central Conservatory of Music as a guest lecturer, and paved the way for young Chinese composers to study in the United States, including Zhou Long and Chen Yi, who entered Columbia University's Doctor of Musical Arts (DMA) program in 1985 and 1986, respectively (Chang, 2006, p. 41).

Steeped in Chinese philosophy and aesthetics, Chou reintroduced Chinese ancient artistic and literary traditions to a young generation that had been forbidden to study them.[7] In so doing, he put them in touch with the ethos of Chinese artistry. Chou states: "Contrary to Western practice, Chinese traditional art theory does not limit itself to the investigation of materials and structure of any particular art form. It is concerned with concept and perception, how philosophy and aesthetics interpret nature, and the human response to nature; and then how such concerns are expressed in each of the art forms" (Chou, 2007, pp. 503–504).

Chou's compositional philosophy and influence on the "New Wave" generation owe much to his mentor, teacher, and colleague, Edgard Varèse. Known as the "Father of Electronic Music," Varèse shaped Chou's musical vision and engagements as a teacher and cultural ambassador. Chou drew from Varèse's treatment of sound "as living matter" and "musical space as open rather than bounded" (Chou, 1966, p. 1). Varèse's mission was to liberate sound and to explore new instrumental possibilities in the electronic realm: "Our musical alphabet must be enriched. We also need new instruments very badly .... In my own works, I have always felt the need for new mediums of expression ... which can lend themselves to every expression of thought and can keep up with thought" (Chou, 1966, p. 1). Varèse believed that treating sound as "living matter" with the "perfect control of its quality, intensity, and pitch" would yield new "auditory perspectives" with "entirely new combinations of sound ... creating new emotions" (Chou, 1966, pp. 1–2). He also elevated the independence of percussion instruments, adding to their vocabulary of timbres, articulations, and endings, and drew attention to rhythm as a "simultaneous interplay of unrelated elements that intervene at calculated, but not regular time lapses" and as "the element of stability, the generator of form" (Chou, 1966, pp. 3–4).

Chou's aesthetic philosophy drew heavily on Varèse's avant-garde ideas, extending them to the Far East once China's doors reopened. Because of Varèse's example, Chou was able to introduce cross-cultural possibilities to his music and his students.[8] He effectively located a nexus for Western avant-garde and Chinese classical expressions by applying Varèse's ideas directly to Chinese musical and aesthetic traditions.

Though educated in the United States, Chou remained deeply attuned to Chinese classical aesthetics. He encouraged Chen and Zhou to draw inspiration

---

[7] One of these traditions is *Guqin* (*Qin* or *ch'in*) music. Also called "music of the sages," it traces its roots to the Zhou Dynasty (1046 BC to 771 BC) and is associated with Confucius and elite Chinese culture.

[8] I have chosen to sidestep the rich ethnomusicological, anthropological, and sociological implications of Chou's cross-cultural synthesis in favor of Varèse's practical influence on Chou's teaching and, in turn, on Chen and Zhou's music.

from the allied arts of ancient Chinese poetry, drawing, and calligraphy (which Mao banned during the Cultural Revolution) even as Zhou and Chen were learning Western harmony, counterpoint, and orchestration at the Central Conservatory of Music. He states:

> Western composers are becoming more and more interested in the interplay of all the properties of sound and the resulting ramifications. In searching for new means of expression, they are advancing beyond the traditional boundaries of the Western polyphonic concept. The more adventurous younger composers already have begun exploring the immense resources in musical expression afforded by controlling and varying the articulation, timbre, and intensity of individual tones – precisely the same resources that have been of primary importance to Eastern Music. (Chou, 1968–9, p. 19)

Calling attention to the importance of single tones as "living matter," Chou asked composers to consider individual tones both for their independent characteristics and value as well as the "state of mind" the performer adopts in producing them (Chou, 1968–9, p. 20). *Guqin* performance practices, with their intricate approach to individual tones – their attack, intensity, and ending – align perfectly with these aesthetic aims, as does their less regularized, organic, and natural approach to rhythm. Other connections include the importance of percussion as an elevated musical entity, the identification of "new instruments" like those found in traditional Chinese ensembles, and music's unbounded connection to other art forms (e.g., the motion of a calligraphy brush or the intonation or rhythm of Chinese speech). Lei Liang, an editor of a Chinese edition of Chou Wen-Chung's writings, recalled Chou's question to his students: "When is a line not a line?" Liang continued, "If you think of a line that is drawn with a pencil or a pen, it is almost an absurd question . . . But if the line is drawn with a brush, it's of course not just a line: It's emotion, it's expression, it encompasses dimensions, even counterpoint . . . [Chou] essentially made himself into a calligrapher with sound" (Da Fonseca-Wollheim, 2019).

Chou's philosophical and interdisciplinary wisdom was formative for Chen and Zhou, who sought an original yet authentic expression reflecting their Chinese heritage and Western modernist training. His appeal for a Chinese modernism informed by the natural world and Chinese philosophy and aesthetics resonated deeply. For Zhou, this meant Tang poetry, *guqin* music, and cross-cultural instrumentations, and for Chen, *Baban*, the Golden Mean, indeterminacy, and serialism.[9] The differences are noteworthy.

---

[9] *Baban* is an ancient folk tune with theoretical significance in its use of eight beats and the presence of the Golden Mean in its structure.

3 Zhou Long

3.1 Family History

The social and political backdrop for both Chen Yi and Zhou Long's early childhood years was one of peace and openness as the turbulence of the Sino-Japanese War (1937–45) and the Communist Revolution (1946–9) subsided. Both were born in 1953 when China's young Communist government was implementing its First Five-Year Plan, a Soviet-inspired rapid industrialization agenda. Along with the development of infrastructure and industrial capacities, the period saw a wave of free expression and thought blossoming during the Hundred Flowers Campaign (1956–7), with Mao lifting bans on intellectuals' freedom of speech. Draconian measures followed with the Anti-Rightist Campaign (1957–9), which punished critics of the state. These precedents were the birth pangs that culminated in the Great Proletarian Cultural Revolution (1966–76), Mao's repressive sociopolitical campaign to eliminate capitalism and traditionalist elements from Chinese society.

Zhou's complex family background, a blend of two worlds – China's past and its future – with landowners on his father's side and Communist revolutionaries on his mother's, profoundly affected his experience of the Cultural Revolution. Zhou's mother, He Gaoyong (1928–86), was the stepdaughter of Zhu De, a military leader, member of the Communist government, and the eventual Chinese House Speaker. Her biological mother, He Zhihua, and Zhu De were among the earliest Chinese students of Marxism in Berlin and Moscow (Figure 2). Returning to China, they became Communist Party members upon the party's establishment in 1921 and helped catalyze the events that led to the Communist Revolution in 1949. Zhu De and He Zhihua eventually had a daughter, Zhu Min, who grew up together with He Gaoyong as half-sisters in Sichuan.

Though Zhou's maternal side was Communist aligned, his paternal grandfather's status as a landowner condemned him to harsh treatment during the Cultural Revolution. (As an adult, Zhou was unable to join the Communist party and the army because of his politically mixed background.) After the Communist Revolution in 1949, landowners, particularly those with laborers, were subject to repression. There were five blacklisted categories of people: *Di* – landlords, *Fu* – the well-to-do, *Fan* – counterrevolutionaries, *Huai* – criminals, and *You* – rightists, who were mostly intellectuals. Among these, the landlords were the most reviled. Zhou's paternal grandfather, Zhou Zanwen, a graduate of Fudan University, owned land in a suburb of Shanghai, and though

Figure 2 He Zhihua and Zhu De (front row center in light clothing), 1923 in Germany (photo courtesy of Zhou Long)

he was a supporter of the revolutionary movement, he and his descendants were placed on the government's blacklist.

He Gaoyong, a soprano singer, showed unwavering devotion to Zhou's musical education. Her own music training was the result of good fortune and natural talent. Without any formal education, she earned admission to the National College of Music in Shanghai at age fourteen because of her beautiful voice. She was also interested in pursuing piano studies, but lacked the money to secure an instrument, so she enrolled as a soprano in the voice department.

At the Shanghai National Music College, which had relocated to Chongqing in Sichuan, He Gaoyong studied under Ying Shang Neng, a graduate of the University of Michigan who introduced Western vocal arts to China. He was a rare exception among the faculty, who were mostly trained in the Russian tradition. At nineteen, He Gaoyong completed her education as a member of the first graduating cohort that eventually laid the pedagogical foundation for China's conservatory-level teaching nationwide. Her colleagues included legends like Yan Liangkun and Luo Zhongrong, two individuals who later played an important role in Zhou's musical development.

Upon graduating, He Gaoyong taught at the Taiwan Normal University, an opportunity arranged by Miao Tianrui, the President of the National Music

College. However, after teaching for only one year, the Communist Revolution erupted in 1949. With the Communist presence established in Beijing, and Chiang Kai-shek's retreat to Taiwan underway, Zhu Min summoned He Gaoyong to return. Upon returning to Beijing, she joined the chorus of the Central Philharmonic Society and eventually taught at the China Conservatory, which had merged with the Central Conservatory of Music. (After the Cultural Revolution, these schools separated, and He Gaoyong transferred to the Central Conservatory of Music.)

Like He Gaoyong, Zhou's father, Zhou Zutai (1920–86), also discovered the arts by chance, but unlike his wife, he was an "educated" man, having attended middle school. While creating posters for the pre-Mao anti-Kuomintang government student movement, he discovered his gift for illustration and drawing. This led him to the Shanghai Academy of Fine Arts and later the National Academy of Art in Hangzhou, where he was classmates with Wu Guanzhong, the father of Chinese modernist painting. After the Communist Revolution in 1949, the central government recruited Zhou Zutai to Beijing to establish the first Department of Stage Design at The Central Academy of Drama, where he taught and led the fine arts department.

Zhou Zutai's introduction to He Gaoyong happened through their mutual connection to Li Ling, the head of the Central Philharmonic Society (orchestra and choir). Li Ling had deep ties to Zhou Zutai's family in Shanghai, having received financial support from Zhou Zanwen to establish a pioneering new music magazine. Li Ling introduced He Gaoyong to Zhou Zutai, and in 1952, they were married in Beijing. Regarding his introverted father, Zhou Long commented, "He could not have found a wife otherwise."

Decades later, well after the Cultural Revolution, Li Ling played another critical role in Zhou's life. On one of Chou Wen-Chung's many exploratory visits to the Central Conservatory as a lecturer and founder of the Center for US-China Arts Exchange, a conversation ensued between Chou and Li about sending talented Chinese composers to Columbia University. Li, the Vice President of the Chinese Musicians Association, recommended Zhou as the first Chinese candidate to apply to Columbia's DMA program. Zhou was accepted and left China for New York City in August 1985.

3.2 Childhood Exposure to Music (1953–1966)

As the son of a musician and a visual artist, Zhou's artistic formation was always interdisciplinary. His father's instruction in theatrical set design, his mother's voice lessons at home, and the conversations on literature and art in his

Figure 3 Zhou Long and Sister Zhou Feng, 1959 in Beijing
(photo courtesy of Zhou Long)

residential community made for rich learning. Though Zhou exhibited neither prodigious talent nor interest in playing an instrument, his sensitivity to voice, visual imagery, design, and sound sharpened.

Zhou began studying the piano at age five (Figure 3), but his real childhood passion was building things – a radio or motorboat – sparking his ambition to become an engineer. Like many mothers, He Gaoyong was challenged by Zhou's refusal to practice. Zhou dutifully executed his Beyer and Czerny exercises for two years and played simple Schumann pieces, Mozart's *Turkish March*, and an arrangement of the *Internationale*, the communist anthem. However, after commencing his formal education at seven, Zhou struck a deal with his mother. He told her, "Either I keep practicing, or I go to school. You can't have both." So, He Gaoyong let him stop the piano.

In the place of piano studies, He Gaoyong demanded that Zhou study Chinese poetry and literature. While living in the faculty housing at The Central Academy of Drama, Zhou was exposed to the teaching of accomplished play-wrights and literature professors. He studied Tang poetry and took English language lessons. Although poetry was at his mother's insistence, this exposure became an important source of inspiration. Zhou also painted between the ages of seven and twelve, having observed his father's studio teaching.

The voice lessons his mother gave at home also left a lasting impression. She instructed students on how to correct their intonation and develop their sound. Zhou described some as sounding "awful." To this day, he remains fastidious about vocal intonation, a characteristic that played a significant role in his choice of singers for his opera, *Madame White Snake*. Zhou stated that regardless of a singer's reputation, he "cannot tolerate intonational errors and the use of a wide vibrato to cover them up." He is similarly careful with instrumentalists and their ability to play in tune.

Zhou credits his mother for his decision to become a composer. As a music lover, she shared her admiration for older colleagues who were composers and conductors. He Gaoyong would say, "My son should become a composer because a composer creates music." To nurture this aspiration, she introduced Zhou to her music colleagues over meals. His aunt Zhu Min, who trained at the Lenin Teachers' College in Moscow and later became a Chinese diplomat at the Cultural Education Council in Moscow, provided recordings of Tchaikovsky and Smetana operas as well as an East German accordion. As a result, Zhou developed a deep love for Russian romantic opera melodies and Western opera in general. Zhou said that the melodic beauty of these operas was imprinted in his childhood psyche and shaped his aesthetic approach to *Madame White Snake*. By crafting beautiful melodies, Zhou kept opera from sounding "ugly."

Before the Cultural Revolution, Western-trained music faculty members such as He Gaoyong were also educated in Chinese folk music. She received instruction on singing styles from Shanxi Province and took up the *banhu* and other traditional instruments. These endeavors exposed Zhou to the styles and sounds of indigenous Chinese music, which were previously foreign to him. Once the Cultural Revolution began, all forms of music making beyond the *yangbanxi* and Mao-inspired works, including folk music, unreformed Beijing opera, and ancient music, were officially prohibited.

3.3 The Cultural Revolution (1966–1976)

When the Cultural Revolution began on May 16, 1966, Zhou Long was thirteen years old and about to enter the No. 23 Middle School in Beijing. The government seized Zhou Zanwen's house and land, destroyed his father's artwork, and sent his parents away to labor on farms, leaving Zhou and his sister at home alone when they were fourteen and ten years old. His No. 23 Middle School class was then sent to work in a steel factory. For over three years, Zhou operated heavy machinery during the night shift, pressing hot steel into thin sheets. Meanwhile, his sister, Zhou Feng (later a costume designer for the Central Ballet in Beijing) attended a youth pioneer program for children, having previously attended the Beijing Jingshan School for gifted students. During this time, Zhou began playing the piano again and improvising themes from the *yangbanxi*. For three years, Zhou only studied Mao's writings, so by the time he was sixteen, he said he had "no knowledge" except for Maoist ideology and how to press steel.

By December 1968, however, Mao released a missive on his reeducation program that changed the course of Zhou's future. "It is very necessary for the urban educated youth to go to the countryside to be re-educated by the poor farmers! ... We must persuade the cadres and others to send their sons and daughters who have graduated from middle school, and university to the countryside. Let's mobilize! The comrades in the countryside should welcome them" (Chen, Fan, Gu, and Zhou, 2020, pp. 3397–3398). The reeducation policy mandated sixteen-year-olds to be sent to the countryside to work on farms unless the family had only one child. Accordingly, Zhou Long was sent 830 miles northeast to remote Heilongjiang near the Soviet border, where conditions were basic and harsh, while his sister Zhou Feng remained in Beijing (Figure 4).

Figure 4 (Left to right) Zhou Zutai, Zhou Long, He Gaoyong, and Zhou Feng, 1968 (photo courtesy of Zhou Long)

Before leaving for Heilongjiang, military delegates from the central government came to Zhou's school to announce the farm assignments. Camp assignments were managed by the middle school and the school district – a local arm of the centralized national system. The officials divided the students into three groups for three different locations based on their families' standing with the government. Those who were more acceptable according to communist ideology were assigned to closer locations such as inner Mongolia (a 4–5-hour train ride from Beijing), where a state-run farm was located. The second group with a less favorable standing was sent northeast to Heilongjiang, and the least acceptable group was sent far south to Yunnan (the most remote location with the harshest conditions) to work on rubber plantations.

The military delegate described Heilongjiang to the students in attractive terms. "We have a dormitory. We have a building. We have secured food for you and cooking oil. We even have a movie theater." Comforted by these words, the fifty students traveled for seventeen hours by train, truck, and tractor-pulled carts and arrived at a state farm in Hegang, a coal city where they were assigned to plant, tend to, and harvest beans, corn, and wheat.

Zhou arrived in Heilongjiang in September 1969, just before National Day on October 1. Though his father was a descendant of a landowner, his employment as a fine arts professor may have kept Zhou from being sent to harsher locations.[10] The remoteness of this farm became apparent once the soldiers transferred the luggage from a truck to tractor-pulled carts. When the tractor-pulled carts arrived at the destination in the woods, all they could see was a large tent. The students wept at the sight of their new home and were reluctant to leave the cart. In response, Zhou played his East German accordion to "make them laugh." Slowly, they regained their composure and disembarked.

Relative to Chen's experiences as a laborer, Zhou's were more difficult because the conditions of this remote assignment were harsher and offered no exposure to music education or performances. The tent housing had a curtain in the center to separate the girls from the boys. Sleeping mats covered the wooden floors with students lined up in rows, and they cooked their meals in an outdoor mud kitchen. Summers were hot and rainy, made worse by the hordes of mosquitoes that kept them awake at night. Winters were extremely harsh – so cold that the toothpaste froze. As a result, Zhou suffered from infections and swelling in his knees.

Zhou was first assigned to the night shift – maintaining security and keeping a wood fire burning continuously in the kitchen to ward off the extreme cold.

---

[10] Zhou shared that there was some unpredictability to these work assignments despite how systematic the process seemed.

Work never stopped. During the winter, when farming was impossible, the youth would build housing and do other light work. Zhou would cook food for the night shift workers who ate upon their return. One night, after cooking pancakes and vegetables, Zhou fell asleep without extinguishing the flames completely, thereby causing a fire. At the morning meeting the next day, he heard about the accident, oblivious to the dramatic events of the previous night. The supervisor subsequently fired Zhou from this duty but assigned him to drive heavy farm equipment in the spring of 1970. Though Zhou was a muscular, stocky youth and well-suited for demanding field labor, the supervisor favored Zhou by giving him this easier assignment. After a period of training, Zhou drove a tractor and combine harvester. He recalled the extremely dusty conditions while seeding wheat and soybeans. By the end of the day, he was covered in dirt. His other daily work chores included carrying 200-pound bags of beans.

Zhou also experienced other forms of stress. As a result of an undeclared military conflict between China and the Soviet Union that began in March 1969, there was heightened tension on both sides of the border. For personal protection, Zhou and his colleagues carried Japanese rifles and flares, knowing that Soviet spies were nearby. For mental relief, he improvised and played revolutionary songs and Russian folk tunes on his East German accordion.

After three years in Heilongjiang, a sudden back injury allowed him to return to Beijing for recovery. With the help of Li Ling's son, Li Xin, Zhou Zutai was able to win his release from Heilongjiang and return to Beijing for one year. During this hiatus, Zhou Long enjoyed the rare privilege of taking private music lessons with He Gaoyong's colleagues and had access to recordings of Western classical works. Unemployed and living in the city, these veteran professors were eager to teach Zhou basic theory, harmony, counterpoint, conducting, orchestration, and later songwriting on a weekly basis. They equipped Zhou with a foundation in tonal music. Li Yinghai and Gu Danru taught him pentatonic and Western harmony (Sposobin's *Uchebnik garmonii*); Luo Zhongrong, theory (Schoenberg's *Harmonielehre*), counterpoint, and orchestration; Yan Liangkun, score-reading and conducting; and Fan Tzuyin, songwriting and accompaniment. Zhou learned how to write two, three, four, and up to eight-part works as well as fugues and absorbed harmonic theory through the Sposobin textbook (the first official harmony textbook approved by the USSR), which he reviewed several times before and during his studies at the Central Conservatory. He remarked that these professors were happy to teach him because he was a "country, not a city boy anymore" and that he became like a "family member" to them. Zhou also had access to recordings obtained from the librarian of the Central Newsreel and Documentary Film

Studio. She supplied Zhou with recordings of the Vienna Boys Choir, Prokofiev's Symphony No. 7, Rachmaninoff's *Symphonic Dances*, and others, as did his aunt Zhu Min, who procured recordings of Russian operas.

With the reeducation policy still in effect, Li Xin facilitated Zhou's transfer to Zhangjiakou (300 miles northwest of Beijing) in 1973 to join the Zhangjiakou Song and Dance Troupe, where he participated until matriculating at the Central Conservatory in the spring of 1978 (admitted fall of 1977). At Zhangjiakou, Zhou's rise was meteoric, as he learned by doing. He began by accompanying singers on his accordion and eventually became a composer, conductor, arranger, and performance organizer for their small orchestra – a Western single wind orchestra combined with *dizi, sheng, erhu, pipa, yangqin,* and *daruan.* He worked with a choral conductor (also a songwriter) on creating musical adaptations of Mao's propaganda directives. Upon receiving a new text, the choral conductor would set the text to music, and Zhou would create an arrangement for the orchestra. Rehearsals would commence the following week for performance. The turnaround time was quick. He also arranged songs for choir and composed short scores for dance that communicated Mao's education agenda. One such work for male dancer, orchestra, and chorus entitled *"Bi ye gui lai"* ("A Graduate Returns Home") depicts the homecoming of a student from the countryside who attended university.[11]

In Zhangjiakou, Zhou also learned a vast array of ethnic music styles that were principally for voice. Three musical genres converged in Zhangjiakou in inner Mongolia – Shanxi opera, Hebei opera, and *Errentai,* a unique Mongolian art form that integrated Shanxi and Hebei influences. *Errentai,* which literally means "two people stage," was a form of light opera accompanied by percussion or instruments with storytelling and conversation between the two persons. This form of entertainment has since receded in popularity, eclipsed by *Errenzhuan,* a similar form of light opera. (Zhou's early work, *Taiping Drum* (1983) for violin and piano, bears the influence of *Errentai* and *Errenzhuan.*) Although Zhangjiakou is in the Hebei province, the accent is heavily influenced by the people of the Shanxi province.

Additionally, the Zhangjiakou Song and Dance Troupe, which reported directly to the municipal cultural bureau, had a folk music research studio. Consequently, Zhou had opportunities to collect folk song materials for study and to do field research. He even returned to Heilongjiang on one such field trip to study the opera tradition of the *Oroqen,* one of the oldest ethnic minorities in northeast China. Exposure to the music and dialects of ethnic minorities

---

[11] Rural youth known as *Gongnongbing xueyuan* – worker-peasant-soldier students" were encouraged to attend university in urban centers even as urban youth were sent to the countryside for reeducation.

Figure 5 Zhou Long in Mongolia, 1976 (photo courtesy of Zhou Long)

sensitized Zhou to the art of notating microtonal inflections in pitch and text. Zhou shared, "As a composer, you have to give very clear directions, because you can't demonstrate to the musicians every time, if you are not there. So, you have to notate it, and we notate it by using some notes or directions . . . For the instrumental and vocal parts, we gave directions on how to mimic the style." Zhou's visit to Inner Mongolia left a strong impression. He recalled learning opera in the Mongolian folk song style and living in a tent with the Mongolian people and observing small children riding horses and singing these folk songs (Figure 5).

3.4 Central Conservatory of Music (1978–1983)

Zhou's work at the Zhangjiakou Song and Dance Troupe put him in a strong position to apply to the Central Conservatory after the Cultural Revolution ended with Mao's death on September 9, 1976. It also prepared him for the cross-cultural instrumentations he pioneered at the Central Conservatory. On a train ride into Beijing, Zhou heard an announcement that universities and conservatories were reopening. He auditioned with his dance score, "*Bi ye gui lai*," for solo male dancer, triple wind orchestra, and sixty-member chorus that was recorded by the Shijiazhuang (capital of Hebei province) opera hall orchestra and chorus for a provincial art festival. In addition, he submitted revolutionary songs set in the *Errenzhuan* style. He described them as tonal folk/pop songs: "All the revolutionary songs sound like Broadway . . . because Madame

Mao knew Broadway. She was an actress in the '30s and '40s ... During the Cultural Revolution, all the songs, chords, and dancing were ... pretty much similar." Zhou added that this adoption of Western musical style was entirely acceptable to the state. What was not acceptable was any hint of experimentalism.

After taking entrance exams, which were reinstated for colleges and universities in 1977 by Vice Premier Deng Xiaoping to rebuild the educational system, Zhou was accepted to the Central Conservatory in the fall of 1977. Several hundred musicians were accepted out of an applicant pool of over approximately 17,000. Among them were thirty-two composers.[12] However, the lack of available student housing resulted in a soft start in the spring semester of 1978, followed by an official opening in the fall. After ten years of closure, the school reopened with little to no resources – the library shelves were bare. Rebuilding the curriculum started from the ground up. Zhou's family friend who worked in the Beijing Film Studio Library supplied him with recordings that included his earliest exposure to twentieth-century Western orchestral works: Stravinsky's *Rite of Spring*, Respighi's *Fountains of Rome* and *Pines of Rome*, and Russian neoclassical works, which made an indelible impression on his musical psyche. The entire class of thirty-two composition and conducting students crowded around the miniature score of the *Rite of Spring* while listening to the recording.

With so little available, Zhou listened to these recordings "a hundred times." Although resources were scarce, he found this "most effective because [when] you really want to learn something, and that's the only material you have ... you get into it." From childhood, Zhou grew up listening to the melodies of Tchaikovsky, Verdi, Puccini, and Smetana, but the exposure to Western orchestral music was completely new. "This [was] the first time we were going to experience it and listen to it. And we were very excited because we [heard] the language. It's really different from ... classical opera." Zhou recalled how difficult it was during the first hearing to follow the metric changes in the score of Stravinsky's *Rite of Spring*. "So, this Stravinsky, the variety of the rhythm changes, we never experienced before. And for myself, Respighi's *Fountains of Rome* and *Pines of Rome*, all of this symphonic sound was to me ... very fresh. I heard some Impressionism also ... but I thought this was more angular." (Zhou happily shared that a critic once described his own works as "angular Impressionism.")

Once at the Central Conservatory, Zhou studied with Su Xia and remained his student for the duration of his bachelor's studies (Figure 6). Su was among the founding faculty members of the Central Conservatory, was head of the

---

[12] For a more detailed account of this composer cohort, see *Chen Yi* by Edwards and Miller, p. 23.

Figure 6 Zhou Long (left) and Su Xia, 2011 in Beijing
(photo courtesy of Zhou Long)

composition department, and taught several successful Chinese art music com
posers by focusing on the fundamentals. Though an accomplished composer, he
was not actively composing by the time Zhou became his student.

Su's teaching of tonal and pantonal works was systematic and disciplined.
Rather than having his students play their compositions for him at the piano, he
would sit at the piano and examine each note, stop after every chord to think
about the voice leading and chord choice, and then delete extraneous pitches.
"He was very critical" and scrutinized the students in and outside of class.
According to Chen Yi, Su went to the library to see who checked out books and
scores and publicly criticized students who had not done so. As a result, his
students were dedicated and composed very clearly and logically.

During the first two years, Zhou worked on small works – first song and
choral writing, then chamber compositions, and only later, large-scale works
like a symphonic poem. His earliest official compositions from these years
include three tonal/pentatonic works: *Song Beneath the Moon* (1978) for piano
(arranged for two *guanzi* and *yangqin*) inspired by a Dai folk song, *Ballade of
the Sea* (1979), a song cycle for soprano and piano based on a text by Tuo
Huang, and *Mongolian Folk-Tune Variations* (1980) for piano. The variations
are based on a pentatonic pastoral folk tune, "*Mongolian Xiao Diao.*" In Zhou's
words: "At that time, I was looking for a theme for the variation[s]. So, I looked
through many folk tunes, and liked this one very much. I thought the major
tunes were not very interesting to me, so I picked a minor tune, a melody in the
key of *Yu* (one of the Chinese pentatonic modes). I thought it was very lyrical,
very open, and I felt there was potential for this theme to become a variation"

(Jiao, 2014, p. 30). The theme, eight variations, and coda display textures that are contrapuntal, through-composed, and lyrical with occasional hints of French Impressionism. A variety of register displacements and accompaniment textures that imitate Chinese instruments are also present. Zhou added, "There are several long-distance modulations. I studied with Su Xia for five years. At that time, he was very strict about it, and very thoughtful. He said you don't have to be too formal. There are some closely related modulations, and you could let it flow. Some modulations are sudden modulations, and some other places are purposefully designed" (Jiao, 2014, p. 35).

As a result of Chou Wen-Chung's teaching visits, which began in 1979, Zhou thought extensively about cross-cultural instrumentation. "I was already interested in exploring some kind of treatment of traditional Chinese instruments using [a] twentieth-century [approach], but I didn't have the resources … So, most of my instrumental compositions are heavily influenced by the ideas and philosophies of Chou Wen-Chung's visits to the Conservatory." Chou used his own compositions to expose Zhou and his colleagues to the ways he adapted the notation and sound of Chinese instruments to Western ones.[13] Zhou stated, "his own music made a more direct impression on me because of his philosophy … the treatment of the Chinese instrument, the cultural background combined with the twentieth-century, and the influence from Varèse." Chou's *Yü Ko*, which is based on an ancient *ch'in* (*qin* or *guqin*) melody from the thirteenth century and adapted for western instruments, strongly influenced Zhou Long's first orchestral work, *Fisherman's Song* (1981), a tone poem. In *Song of Ch'in* (1982) for string quartet, Zhou adapted *qin* music with its plucked textures, ornamentation, registral span, and timbres for string quartet. *Guqin* music also influenced Zhou's *Guang Ling San Symphony* (1983) for large orchestra, inspired by a pre–Tang Dynasty legend about a swordsmith. Barbara Mittler describes Zhou's early works such as the *Guang Ling San Symphony* and the *Dong Shi xiao pin* ("Dong Shi knits her brows") ballet (1983), as incorporating "elements of early modernism (especially Stravinsky) and pentatonic romanticism" (Mittler, 1997, p. 168). His 1983 graduation recording, entitled "*Guang Ling San*," on the China Record Company label, includes these major works: *Guang Ling San* Symphony (1983), *Fisherman's Song* (1981) for orchestra, and the ballet *Dong Shi* (1983). One other significant work from this period is *Words of the Sun* (1982) for mixed chorus – an impressionistic work based on the poetry of Nobel Prize nominee Ai Qing.

The resumption of cultural exchange and visits from foreign ensembles after the Cultural Revolution exposed Zhou to other cross-cultural innovations that

---

[13] Chou also introduced other works by Elliott Carter and George Crumb.

inspired new explorations. Zhou recalled a visit by a Japanese traditional instrumental ensemble (e.g., *shakuhachi* and *koto*) and its modernist approach to this traditional medium that "really opened up [his] mind." It was this combination of a modernist style in the context of a traditional performance genre that later inspired Zhou to compose *Valley Stream* (1983), his first work for a Chinese ensemble: *dizi, guan, zheng,* and percussion. (Su suggested the name "*Hongguliushui,*" which means a stream flowing into a stream. Zhou said this imagery shaped the work.)

Zhou pioneered new sonic experiences by introducing Western percussion, mainly vibraphone and glockenspiel, into the traditional Chinese ensemble. "[It was] the first time in history because nobody had done this before." He said that today the piece sounds like a folk song work, but at the time was new – a complete break from tradition. "The audience was not used to it" because the sound was "not traditional enough." This was one of the earliest signs of Zhou's inclination to innovate and push the boundaries in his modernism. Zhou described his approach as "revolutionary" – something others felt "went a bit too far," and credits Chou Wen-Chung for this experiment because he shared Varèse's innovations with percussion in works like *Ionisation* (1931).

A Canadian percussion ensemble's visit to the Central Conservatory also inspired Zhou's later composition, *Triptych of Bell-Drum Music* (1984), the first work in China for solo percussion. The work employs a set of percussion instruments, including bronze bells and stone chimes for one player. At this point in his conservatory training, he was "crazy" about percussion. In Zhou's mind, the colorful use of percussion "made a work sound more modern." In *Fisherman's Song,* he employed a battery of percussion instruments such as wood blocks, tom toms, and Chinese cymbals. For his award-winning *Wu Kui* (1983), a solo piano piece composed for a pedagogical works competition, Zhou treated the piano as a percussion instrument in the manner of Bartók, with frequent meter changes to depict the celebratory folk dance of the Manchu people that he had witnessed as a member of the Zhangjiakou Song and Dance Troupe. In the score's preface, Zhou writes that "capturing the original style of this dance, this solo piano piece opens with animated rhythmic patterns, moves into a slower, free-flowing and lyrical middle section, and concludes with a return to the fierce exultant rhythms and motifs of the beginning" (Zhou, 2002, p. 2). Unlike the regularized rhythms of the dance, he introduces "irregular rhythmic patterns" (Jiao, 2014, pp. 52–53) and imitates Chinese drums to drive the energy of the work. Treating the piano as a percussion instrument began with this work and continued in subsequent solo works. His *Taiping Drum* (1983) for violin and piano, a tonal yet modernist work, also explores a range of percussive (Bartók-like) treatments in combination with evocative melodies.

Although Zhou explored sonic and timbral possibilities through these cross-cultural treatments, he also discovered an opportunity to develop a truly free rhythm, an underdeveloped element in Chinese music. For this he turned to *guqin*. *Guqin* music was notated using fingerings on a *qin* tablature, and realizing these fingerings (which produce specific character qualities) involves their translation into pitches, a process known as *dapu*. Though *dapu* informs the pitches, it does not indicate durations. Every *guqin* master uses an individualized rhythmic approach guided by the character of the music, a central aspect of *guqin* interpretation. Furthermore, there are different schools of *guqin* interpretation – the more rhythmically active approach of the north versus the more relaxed, gentle interpretations of the south. The limitations of Western rhythmic notation force a composer to choose between precise metric and rhythmic values to notate every change or adopting a looser notation that captures the spirit of the music. At first, Zhou preferred to notate the rhythms precisely, but this presented difficulties. The challenge is, "the different rhythmic treatments really make the music a different piece with a different spirit." Zhou said some composers who use a fully notated approach explore metric changes for every bar, to which he responds, "You are fooling yourself . . . you have a 3/8, 5/8, and 9/8 meter, but the pulse is in eighth notes. Nobody can tell which measure is five, which is nine, and so on. It is just an eighth-note pulse . . . like a march . . . It seems like variety, but it sounds the same."

Zhou also underwent rigorous and systematic studies of Chinese traditional music, something he noted is not done to the same degree in Chinese conservatories today. These courses continued for two to three years and covered the various regions of China from different periods and the many ethnic minorities like the Miao in the south, the Uyghurs in the northwest, and the Mongolians in the north. Local opera, with its varied styles of dialogue and storytelling, and ensemble music, with its different instrumentation and playing styles, were also part of the curriculum. He had to memorize the regional folk songs and learn to pronounce the various dialects and languages.

Exposure to ethnic music continued beyond the classroom during the summers. Though Zhou had already experienced fieldwork in the north (Heilongjiang) as a member of the Zhangjiakou Song and Dance Troupe, conservatory training facilitated additional visits to other regions. He traveled to the mountainous regions of Guangxi to study the music of the Dong and Yao minorities and Guizhou for the Miao minority as well as to Fujian on China's southeastern coast. For this fieldwork, Zhou and his colleagues used Arabic numerals instead of Western notation (twelve half-steps) to document the music due to the many microtonal inflections. Number notation with arrows going up or down indicated quarter-tone shifts in either direction to capture the singing style with its "heavy vibrato." A cassette recording device also helped students revisit the songs for more accurate transcription later. Inspired by his exposure to these traditions, Zhou composed his *Partita* for violin and piano (1983, rev. 2000), a four-movement work based on original mountain and work song melodies from Northern China.

3.5 China National Broadcasting Corporation (1983–1985)

Upon graduating from the Central Conservatory in 1983, Zhou decided to work rather than continue studying. He became a member of the creative studio in the radio division of China's National Broadcasting Corporation (CNBC) as the composer-in-residence for the National Broadcasting Symphony Orchestra. At that time, one's workplace was determined by the government. In Zhou's words, "It [was] the highest national organization" of employment, and his assignment the most coveted for a young composer. He earned a salary, worked from home with flexible hours, and had full access to the recording and performance studios in the National Ministry.

As a composer-in-residence, Zhou gained greater hands-on experience composing and recording for the Corporation's mixed Western and Chinese ensembles (Figure 7). On occasion, "the broadcasting, television station ... wanted signature music to open the program. They want fourteen or twenty seconds of orchestral music ... and you write the signature music." Overnight, a few copyists would create parts for the orchestral musicians, and the next morning at ten o'clock, the musicians would assemble in the studio to record the work for broadcast. This recalled his work at the Zhangjiakou Song and Dance Troupe, where he composed works for immediate rehearsal and performance.

Zhou's pioneering approach to cross-cultural instrumentation and expression continued to flourish in chamber music as well. He composed *Green* (1984) for bamboo flute and *pipa* (arranged for soprano and *pipa* in 1991), a poignant vocalise for instruments. At the request of *guqin* master Wu Wenguang, Zhou composed *Su* (1984) for flute and *qin* (arranged for flute, harp, and *pipa* in 1990). It is a modernist setting of the first known *qin* melody, "Secluded Orchid." This Tang Dynasty melody, influenced by Persian music of that era, uses the eleven-note Persian scale from four thousand years ago.[14] Zhou was also the first Chinese composer to write a solo work for a full battery of percussion instruments, *Triptych of Bell-Drum Music* (1984). With three movements, the first features drums; the second, pitched instruments like bronze

---

[14] Persians introduced the *pipa* (Chinese lute) to China.

Figure 7 Zhou Long in his CNBC studio in Beijing, 1984
(photo courtesy of Zhou Long)

bells, stone chimes (jade), glockenspiel, and vibraphone; and the third, wooden instruments like Chinese tom toms and wood blocks. These works were broadcast on Radio Beijing and released in a 1984 recording entitled "Valley Stream" (China Record Company label), which included *Song Beneath the Moon* (1978), *Valley Stream* (1983), *Green* (1984), and *Triptych of Bell-Drum Music* (1984). This was followed by a second recording from a Radio Beijing broadcast consisting of the *Song of Ch'in* (1982), *WuKui* (1983), and other chamber works. Zhou mentioned that his assignment at CNBC and these two professional recordings were rare accomplishments for a young composer, and that they opened the doors to his next opportunity, doctoral training at Columbia University.

Zhou's decision to leave CNBC was a difficult one. He felt free to explore musical ideas without drawing unwanted political scrutiny given music's abstract nature. Additionally, China was a more open society after the Cultural Revolution, and composers from the United States and Europe were visiting and enjoying cultural and intellectual exchange. However, exposure to Western thinking at the Central Conservatory had given Zhou a taste of new possibilities. He felt that leaving China was crucial for his growth as a composer. Had he stayed, he would have become "rich" from creating soundtracks for television and musical transitions for radio broadcasts, but his own personal style would not have developed. Despite the privileged nature of the CNBC assignment and Zhou's satisfaction with the post, he left to pursue more advanced compositional skills. "I was just not satisfied with my knowledge."

The one challenge was that Zhou Long and Chen Yi were married on July 20, 1983 but not equally prepared to leave. Chen was pursuing a master's degree in composition at the Central Conservatory and serving as a representative to the People's Congress in Beijing. With one year remaining in her graduate program, Chen stayed in China, and Zhou Long headed for the United States. He said the opportunity to study with the exceptional faculty at Columbia and experience New York City's thriving cultural life was too tempting to turn down.

3.6 Doctoral Program at Columbia University (1985–1993)

Just as the exceptional recording opportunities at the Zhangjiakou Song and Dance Troupe positioned him well for admission to the Central Conservatory, the two professional recordings from his work at CNBC made possible his admission to Columbia's DMA program. In 1985, Zhou became the first student from the Central Conservatory to study in the United States, having been recruited by Chou Wen-Chung. Though Zhou did not complete a master's degree program nor achieve a TOEFL (Test of English as a Foreign Language) score, he successfully gained acceptance based on his recorded works.

Adjusting to American life, however, was a challenge. Zhou said he was in a state of "culture shock," that he was slow to acquire English, and felt isolated, since few other students from China were present at that time. Also, Zhou's modest resources were stretched by New York City's high cost of living. He wanted to return to China badly, but every evening, he visited art galleries and attended theater, dance, and music performances that "opened [his] eyes." The city afforded an artistic immersion that simply wasn't available in Beijing.

Zhou said he had formative philosophical conversations with Chou about style and cultural synthesis, completed composition exercises, and made forays into atonality. Because Chou was not satisfied with Zhou's earliest attempts at atonal writing, he introduced him to the ideas and works of other Asian composers, such as Tōru Takemitsu and Isang Yun. He insisted that "As a Chinese composer, you cannot just dig into the Chinese tradition … you really have to know what happened in East Asian culture." Despite Chou's help, Zhou said the challenges of the cultural transition made it difficult to create new music. He could not "really concentrate nor compose for almost two years."

The one work he did complete during these first two years was for Music From China, a New York City–based organization (founded in 1984) that promoted music for traditional Chinese ensembles, including contemporary compositions. Zhou composed a traditional pentatonic work – *The Moon Rising High* (1986) for pipa and traditional ensemble (*dizi, daruan, yangqin, zheng, erhu,* and percussion), as his first submission. Beginning in 1987, Zhou served as music director of this ensemble for over thirty years, premiering works annually at New York City's Merkin Hall. The following year, Music From China commissioned Zhou to compose the more modernist work *Heng* ("*Eternity,*" 1987) for *dizi, pipa, yangqin, zheng, erhu,* and percussion. Zhou describes *Moon Rising High* and *Heng* as works he was comfortable writing for traditional instruments. Music From China subsequently commissioned works for mixed ensembles of Chinese and Western instruments. Zhou's work in the traditional Chinese instrumental medium was continuous and encouraged by his involvement with this organization. Other works in this category include *Variations on a Poetess' Lament* (1989) for a traditional Chinese instrumental ensemble and fixed media and *A Poetess' Lament* for soprano, *pipa, zheng,* and *erhu* (1989, revised 2000).

By 1990, however, Zhou increasingly blended Western and Eastern instrumentations or continued developing techniques for Western instruments to mimic the sounds and textures of Chinese traditional instruments. *Pipa Ballad* (text by Bai Juyi, 1991) for soprano, *pipa,* and cello, which uses a Cantonese melody, and *Shi Jing Cantata* (text from the *Book of Songs,* 1990) for soprano, flute, oboe, clarinet, bassoon, strings, and piano (with two sections available as *Two Poems* for mixed chorus) are examples of this. The cantata, however, does not employ a Chinese tune but rather an original modernist melody, thus departing from his normal practice. Other mixed works include *You Lan* for *erhu* and piano (1991), *King Chu Doffs His Armor* (1991), a tonal concerto for *pipa* and orchestra (also arranged for *pipa* and traditional instruments orchestra), and *Tian Ling* ("Nature and Spirit"), a more dissonant work for *pipa* and fourteen Western instruments. The crowning example of Western and Eastern instrumental interchangeability appears in *Da Qu* (1991), a concerto for Chinese percussion and Hong Kong Chinese traditional orchestra that he adapted for Western instruments later that same year.[15] This facile approach is also present in his *Secluded Orchid* (1992), an arrangement of *You Lan* for violin, cello, and piano, later arranged for *pipa, erhu,* cello, and percussion (2000). Known as one of the oldest known *guqin* pieces, Zhou explores the sound of this ancient instrument through extended techniques, including fingernail pizzicati, glissando-pizzicati, stopped string vibrations in the piano, and harmonics. *Wild Grass* (1993) for cello, which Zhou also adapted for solo viola that same year, demonstrates his treatment of Western instruments as *guqin* with the use of pizzicati and glissandi.

---

[15] His doctoral dissertation was a comparison of these two treatments.

While building on these cross-cultural adaptations in his compositions, Zhou felt a need to break away from the familiar and dive into avant-garde explorations more intentionally by 1987. Buddhist, Taoist, and Confucian influences dominated his thinking, brought on by the "culture shock" and "homesickness" he experienced once he arrived in New York City and made worse by the loss of his mother and father in 1986. Zhou said, "I started to question myself. If I study in the States, should I keep doing what I have done before … or discover something new?" This introspection led to the more dissonant work *Soul* (1987) for string quartet (later adapted for *pipa* and string quartet in 1992) and *Wuji* (1987) for piano and fixed media, his most radical experimentations with the "new." *Wuji* was inspired by Mario Davidovsky's *Synchronisms* for the same instrumentation and expresses the Taoist concept of limitlessness (*Wu* – without, *ji* – limits).

Wuji (1987) was commissioned by Harold Lewin, a Manhattan-based pianist with expertise in piano and electronic music, after he heard electronically synthesized Dunhuang ethnic dance music that Zhou wrote for a mutual friend entitled, *Flying Apsaras of Dunhuang* (1986). For *Wuji*, Zhou used a synthesizer – the Yamaha DX7 (a first-generation MIDI keyboard) and a sequencer to create percussive sounds and those of instruments like the Japanese *koto*, which is like the *zheng*. The MIDI's sequencer created "amazing rhythmic patterns" that were randomized. Zhou layered sixteen tracks of recorded material using an eight-track cassette recorder and a mixer. Although Lewin did not ultimately perform the piece because the randomized rhythms were too complex and lacked cues for the pianist,[16] *Wuji* opened his mind to new rhythmic possibilities. Zhou stated, "I'm not good with pitches. Chen Yi is very good with pitches, but I am very interested in rhythm." As a result, Zhou created later versions of this work (absent fixed media) for *zheng*, piano, and percussion (1991), and finally, piano and percussion (2000). Unlike the piano with fixed media score, which has no bar lines, Zhou notated the rhythms and meter for these later versions. This transcription work inspired Zhou, opening possibilities of metric and rhythmic variety that he had not previously considered (an interest that began in 1978 with his first exposures to Stravinsky.)

His work with Mario Davidovsky also coincided with a class on twentieth-century composition taught by a visiting professor, Martha Hyde, marking a creative turning point. Zhou indicated that Columbia was "dominated by the Second Viennese School" during his time. *Ding (Samadhi)* (1988) for clarinet,

---

[16] Xi Wang, a master's degree candidate at the University of Missouri, Kansas City, premiered *Wuji* for a Music Nova concert at UMKC in 2002.

double bass, and percussion, which he later arranged for clarinet, *zheng*, and double bass and dedicated to Davidovsky, was the result of this serial influence. (This work earned first prize from the Ensemble in Mönchengladbach, Germany in 1990.) Zhou defines the work's Buddhist connotations as "the perfect absorption of thought into the one object of meditation." A twelve-tone melody and tonal melody are cast in an abstract improvisational style at "slow speed" with the use of instrumental techniques such as blowing (clarinet), striking (percussion), and bowing (double bass), and a wide span of registers "from very high to very low" (Zhou, 2005, p. 2).[17] Microtonal grace notes dot the texture to evoke the sound effects of traditional Chinese instruments (Zhou, 2005, p. 2). Although *Ding* is Zhou's only serial work, it freed him to explore new approaches more boldly. His *Li Sao Cantata* (1988) for soprano and fourteen-member orchestra, based on the poetry of Qu Yuan, is a completely atonal work with a modernized musical style. Zhou said that the use of voice and Chinese poetry demanded greater flexibility, so he abandoned serialism in favor of free atonality to better capture the inflection and intonation of the Chinese text. With this work, Zhou decided never to return to the pentatonic music he had composed while in China – You simply "can't recite [in Chinese] using the pentatonic [scale]," given the microtonal nature of the Chinese language.

After gaining new insights from *Wuji* and *Ding*, Zhou felt confident to carry on with this overtly spiritual creativity. *Dhyana* (1990), a quintet for flute, clarinet, violin, cello, and piano, references the deepest meditative states in Buddhist practice that Zhou turned to during his early years in the United States. Zhou's program notes state:

> The inspiration for *Dhyana* comes from the Buddhist concept of 'cultivation of thought' – the process of gathering scattered thoughts and focusing them on one object to arrive at enlightenment. To express the progression from worldliness to serenity and, finally, to purification, the musical structure moves from complex to simple in pitch, from dense to relaxed in rhythm, from tight to open in range, from colorful to monochrome in timbre, from foreground to background in sonority (Green, 2007, p. 549).

In Communist China, Zhou's generation had little knowledge of or experience with Asian philosophical or spiritual traditions (Green, 2007, p. 548). So, Zhou immersed himself in a central Buddhist concept, one that is embedded in the work: the inextricable oneness of opposition and unity – the "unchanging" and "ever-changing" or "fixity" and "unceasing variability" (Green, 2007, 550). These contrasts are manifest, for example, through the juxtaposition of dynamic

---

[17] Zhou analyzed *Ding* in its use of serial techniques for the Central Conservatory's Magazine in 1991.

contrasts (e.g., fp to ppp), register jumps versus static pitches, "foreground versus background treatments," or "emptiness" vs. "definiteness" (Green, 2007, pp. 549–552). Zhou described the musical process as one without tonal harmonic progressions or continuity of melodic line. Rather, he adopted a pointillistic texture reminiscent of Webern but with inflections and *portamenti* that suggest the influence of Chinese instruments.

Zhou identified 1987 to 1995 as his most modern or experimental period. It began with *Soul* (1987) for string quartet and ended with *Poems from Tang* for string quartet and orchestra (1995). Although the titles of the movements and inspiration for this later work come from ancient Chinese poetry by well-known poets and *guqin* music, it is modernist in its use of pointillism, dissonance, and abrasiveness.[18] The one exception to this is the second movement, *Fisherman's Song*, which is based on his earlier symphonic poem by the same name from 1981. Zhou's training at Columbia and his transition to life in America significantly influenced these experimentations. Once he completed his doctorate in 1993 and began freelancing, his compositional output slowed. In his words, "not much commission[ing] ... happened." He candidly acknowledged that he was beholden to other parties and their requirements once he started receiving requests. For this reason, "I didn't really go to modernism ... in the end."

4 Chen Yi

4.1 Family History

Chen's family, like Zhou's, was invested in the arts. Early music training was no accident but an integral part of her life alongside an exceptional immersion in Western thought, culture, and language reaching back two generations. According to Chen, her Eurocentric upbringing was very unusual at that time. As a result of her parents' interests, their global perspective, and her exposure to international figures through her father's work, Chen's aesthetics and creative motivations were informed by a transnationalist spirit.

Her pediatrician mother, Dr. Du Dianqin (1919–2012), and internist father, Dr. Chen Ernan (1919–90), were avid amateur musicians who immersed their children in Eurocentric classical music from birth (Figure 8). Du was an accomplished pianist and accordionist and Chen, a violinist and record collector. All three children in her family: Chen Yi, her pianist sister Chen Min (b. 1951), and her violinist brother Chen Yun (b. 1955), became professional

---

[18] Poem titles: I. "Hut Among the Bamboo" by Wang Wei, II. "Fisherman's Song" by Liu Zongyuan, III. "Hearing the Monk Xun Play the Qin" by Li Bai, IV. "Song of Eight Unruly Tipsy Poets" by Du Fu.

Figure 8 (Left to right) Chen Yun, Du Dianqin, Chen Yi, Chen Ernan, and Chen Min, 1957 (photo courtesy of Chen Yi)

musicians. Chen Min, a child prodigy and later concert pianist, performed for Liu Shaoqi, the Vice Chairman of the Communist Party (Edwards and Miller, 2020, p.8).[19] Chen Yun graduated from the Central Conservatory of Music in 1982 and is currently a professor in violin and chamber music at the Central Conservatory.

Chen's parents' commitment to their children's education outside of school was notable and encouraged by her grandparents' immersion in Western culture, faith, and language. Du's parents, who lived in Chaozhou in the countryside of Guangdong province, attended a Baptist missionary school and taught basic subjects like music and literature to school-aged children and youth. Du was a practicing Baptist as was Chen Ernan upon marriage, and the tradition continues for Du's brother and his son, both Baptist ministers. As a child, Chen Yi attended church regularly with her parents, listened to hymns, and read the Bible.

Her father's side of the family was highly educated but not religious. Also residing in Guangdong, Chen Ernan's father was the treasurer for Shantou Customs, overseeing imports and exports. He sent Chen Ernan to elite primary and middle schools in Shanghai, where he also attended a mission school and learned English. Du Dianqin and Chen Ernan met at Lingnan University for medical school. (Du, a pediatrician, was the only female graduate in the class of seven.) Following the 1937 Japanese

---

[19] This impacted the family after Liu fell from grace in 1966.

invasion, Chen Ernan's father left for Hong Kong, but Chen Ernan remained in Guangzhou to establish and run hospitals. By the end of World War II, Chen had established two medical centers: the Huaying Hospital and the Shameen Clinic on Shamian Island.

At the Shameen Clinic, Chen Ernan enjoyed close ties with foreign service officials from the West. Shamian Island, an alluvial sandbar located within Guangzhou City, was home to numerous consulates including those of the United States, Soviet Union, Poland, France, Germany, Australia, Vietnam, and Japan. As a primary school student, Chen Yi welcomed foreign dignitaries at the airport and met a broad audience of listeners through Chen Min's radio, television, and concert performances. She recalls gifts of oversized picture books and stories in different languages being sent to her home in appreciation. Formative interactions with the West also came through Dr. Chen's patients, many of whom were consular officials from around the world.

Chen's daily exposure to the West, the result of her parents' work lives and their interests and colorful dispositions, was exceptional in China. Both Chen Ernan and Du Dianqin were outgoing and "loved life." They were curious, had a wide range of interests, and were driven by the joy of helping others, which brought them into contact with many people. Every day at lunch, Chen Yi and her siblings would listen to recordings of classical music while Chen and Du discussed their patients, emergency room events, medication dosages, and current events that took place all over the world.

Chen absorbed her parents' way of life. Her global perspective, cultural awareness, and desire to help others stand out. When her parents walked the streets of Guangzhou, former patients would call out, "Dr. Du! Dr. Chen!" As a child, Chen understood that these were the voices of the patients her parents had saved. With an energetic and joyful disposition, Chen shared, "Action and behavior are more important than words because I learned from what I have seen … Everywhere I go, I help all my classmates and col-leagues, poor people around me, and all others in society." These expres-sions of altruism shaped Chen's priorities as a musician and had real implications for her experiences during the Cultural Revolution and after.

4.2 Childhood Exposure to Music (1953–1966)

Chen's musical talent appeared early on (Figure 9). Her fluency in piano and violin, which were fostered by lessons as a preschooler, encouraged the devel-opment of a highly sensitized ear[20] and an equally strong aptitude for academic

---

[20] Current research suggests that early music training develops absolute pitch. See Sakakibara, 2014.

Figure 9 Chen Yi, 1961 (photo courtesy of Chen Yi)

work. The combination of these aptitudes with early instrumental instruction, the influence of life-long mentors, and rich learning at home set Chen up for rapid progress and, eventually, specialization.

Early music instruction began with key mentors who provided a well-rounded musical training. She had weekly piano lessons at the age of three with Li Suxin, who taught at the Guangzhou Academy of Music (currently the Xinghai Conservatory), and violin lessons twice weekly at age four with Zheng Rihua and on occasion Zheng Zhong, when Rihua was unavailable. With their help, Chen played in string ensembles made up of adults, teens, and Chen Yun at the local church. (To this day, Chen Yi is fluent as a violinist and able to sight-read complex scores.) These brothers played a central role in Chen's violin and music training for nearly twenty years (with only a three-month interruption at the start of the Cultural Revolution and from 1968–70) until Chen entered the Central Conservatory of Music in the spring of 1978.

Chen was also one of the fortunate few to listen regularly to works from the Western canon. Her father's collection of recordings, Hollywood films, and international melodies that consulate and foreign service officers shared, and music from live performances, including symphony concerts, filled Chen's world. She watched the *Swan Lake* ballet with Galina Ulanova when the Bolshoi Theatre visited and viewed ballet and folk dances from Japan, Romania, and Africa. According to Chen, she was "one in ten thousand" children in Guangdong Province to have had such experiences.

She benefitted from her father's interests in other ways, too. As an amateur violinist fluent in English, Chen Ernan worked with local violin makers such as Liang Guohui, to prepare instruments for international competitions. Translating documents from English to Chinese, Chen Ernan helped these craftspeople learn from international printed resources and test the instruments behind a curtain. He also learned the intricacies of violin making – the finish, craft, and design – knowledge he would share with Chen Yi. Chen Ernan also knew a lot about the violinists who visited China during the 1940s and 1950s and would discuss them in detail with Zheng Rihua while Chen Yi listened.

Though her exposure to Western music was relatively vast, Chen recalled having limited exposure to Chinese indigenous music as a youngster. The family's maid, Huang Li, enjoyed listening to Cantonese opera on the radio while mopping the floors and doing the laundry (Edwards and Miller, 2020, p. 8). Her storytelling and sharing of this style were an introduction to the rich repository of indigenous music that would blossom for Chen during the Cultural Revolution and after. Chen recalls that her mother so disliked hearing this music that she would go to her room and shut the door.

The richness of Chen's musical learning was matched by that of her formal academic education. Chen attended a primary school on Shamian Island dedicated to gifted students that condensed a six-year curriculum into five. As a result, she received a year of education at the No. 29 Middle School, something Zhou Long missed, having attended the six-year primary school program. Chen said she was fortunate to "catch the last train for [a middle school] education before the Cultural Revolution." She received top grades in mathematics, literature, and other subjects including physical education, and she was a leader in her class, answering questions and doing math calculations at the blackboard for public demonstration. In every regard, Chen was a model student, a reputation she maintained during the entirety of her formal education.

The interruption of her schooling caused by the Cultural Revolution in 1966 dashed Chen's parents' dreams for their children's future careers in medicine. Since formal medical training was no longer available, they turned instead to autodidactic disciplines. Chen Yi frequently mentioned the Zheng brothers and the role apprenticeship and private study played in her formation. However, it was Chen Ernan's frequent talks about composers (Mozart, Beethoven, Kreisler, and more) that encouraged Chen Yi to become a composer. While listening to Irish folk songs that Heifetz adapted for the violin or Kreisler's works for violin and orchestra, Chen Ernan would say, "Hey, one day, my daughter will also become a composer who can . . . play her own works."

4.3 The Cultural Revolution (1966–1976)

Though the government's perceptions of Chen's family affected her labor assignments and experience of the Cultural Revolution, unanticipated events facilitated her growth as a musician and composer. As with Zhou, suspicions about Chen's family background arose in the years leading up to the Revolution in 1966. In the late 1950s, Chen Ernan ran the No. 3 People's Hospital, the result of a merger between the Shameen (later Shamian) Clinic on Shamian Island and several other local facilities (Edwards and Miller, 2020, pp. 6–7). During the Anti-Rightist Campaign (1957–9), he lost his position at the hospital, and the family experienced what would later become the Cultural Revolution's standard practices – home searches, confiscations, and identity checks.

In 1965, when Chen applied to a secondary school affiliated with the South China Normal University, her family's categorization as *you* or rightist in the *di fu fan huai you* class system led to her rejection (Edwards and Miller, 2020, pp. 10–11). Chen attended No. 29 Middle School in Guangzhou instead. During World War II, Chen Ernan had driven an ambulance from Guangzhou City to China's closed border at the request of the President of Lingnan University Medical School to facilitate a farewell meeting between an important official from the West and his dying brother. This act of service together with the Chen parents' fluency in English, their connections with friends and patients from foreign consulates, and their receiving of medical supplies from the British Red Cross prompted accusations of their being "suspected international spies." This label persisted for eighteen years until Mao's death in 1976.

The same year that Chen began middle school, Mao issued Order 626, which mandated urban physicians to train rural "barefoot doctors" (Edwards and Miller, 2020, p. 11). Chen Ernan left for the countryside (returning home on weekends) to serve at the Shiling Commune Clinic (Huaxian County). Eventually, he became the associate director of the Huaxian County Hospital and served numerous villagers – saving many farmers' lives. Though difficult, this remote assignment likely spared Chen Ernan's life, since he avoided the anti-intellectual destruction and violence that ensued in major cities, including Guangzhou (Edwards and Miller, 2020, p. 11).

On August 8, 1966, Mao launched the Great Proletarian Cultural Revolution with his Sixteen Articles. Students were instructed to destroy the Four Olds – the old ideas, old culture, old customs, and old habits of the "exploiting class" (De Bary and Lufrano, 2000, pp. 474–475). Radicalized youth known as Red Guards entered Tiananmen Square ready to fight. They attacked, killed, and publicly criticized intellectuals and those associated with the West. In addition, they destroyed historical and cultural sites, artworks, and books. They entered

Chen's home but did not commit acts of violence against her parents due to their years of medical service.

It was during this time that Chen and her classmates from No. 29 Middle School left for the countryside to harvest crops, but after ten days, she came down with a kidney infection that required hospitalization and several months of bed rest. Du continued seeing patients at the hospital and taught her children literature and music at home. She also had a colleague from the Chaozhou village whose children tutored Chen Yi and Chen Yun on a weekly basis in German, English, and Japanese. Du copied the Japanese textbook, which Chen Yi typed in its entirety, since no copy machines were available. She also had access to many English novels supplied by a family friend. Du supplemented this collection with books from the hospital library, enabling Chen and her brother to read many of the classic Chinese novels and poems. Du also continued her children's Western musical training by dampening the sound of their Zimmermann upright piano, placing mutes on their violins, and drawing the curtains. Of her own volition, Chen gathered all the music scores and read through them. She learned to play works such as the 24 Paganini *Caprices*, the Bruch and Mendelssohn violin concertos, and Saint-Saëns' *Introduction and Rondo Capriccioso*.

This music instruction was a precarious pursuit given the scrutiny Du was under. Local workers criticized her authority and practices of encouraging hard work and excellence at the Shameen Clinic and No. 3 Hospital. Political authorities at the hospital later imprisoned Du for ten months. No longer able to practice medicine, she performed hard labor and was "subjected to demoralizing public self-criticism sessions" (Edwards and Miller, 2020, p.14).

By September 1968, another wave of violence erupted as invaders from the Revolutionary Committee broke into the Chen home, destroying and scattering their possessions on the floor (Edwards and Miller, 2020, p. 13). Previous raids, including one during the Anti-Rightist Campaign in 1958, resulted in the confiscation of valuable items. This time, they left the home in ruins but failed to check the piano bench that Chen resolutely sat on containing classical music scores (Edwards and Miller, 2020, p. 13). The purpose of these raids was to subject the family to public humiliation by seizing and displaying questionable items such as her father's LP collection.

Shortly after the raid, students were assigned to groups to fulfill Mao's "sent-down" youth program, which mandated students from urban centers to be reeducated by peasants on farms and in factories. Because Chen was not yet sixteen, she was sent to the suburban No. 64 Middle and High School in Xincun village of the Shimen District, located roughly 100 miles outside of Guangzhou. There she worked barefoot in rice and vegetable fields and learned Maoist doctrine and basic farming science. Chen described herself as a farming "expert." In the winter, she dug the mud from the pond to clean it for the fish that would feed there in the spring. This mineral-rich mud was then used to grow vegetables. She made rows with the soil, distributed the seed, and, once the seed sprouted, she gathered and classified the sprouts, and transplanted them into the muddy water. She grew two types of vegetables and two rounds of rice in a year – one on drier soil and the other in muddy water. In the summers she weeded these plots, stepping barefoot into the water and using her hands to grab the weeds that sprouted between the rice plants. Rice cultivation was central to No. 64 School's reeducation curriculum.

During this time, Chen resided with seven other students in a dormitory room and in the evenings played revolutionary tunes on the violin for local farmers. Folk tunes of the previous feudalistic era and Western music were strictly forbidden, so Chen played revolutionary songs while sitting on her bunk bed. Her first forays into composition began during this period as she adorned these revolutionary and approved folk songs with classical embellishments and virtuosic "Paganiniesque" cadenzas (double stops and runs). On occasion, she practiced her Western classical repertoire.

Then, in 1969, because of mounting tensions between China and the Soviet Union over a border clash on Zhenbao Island (located on the border between Primorsky Krai, Russia, and Heilongjiang Province, China) and a Russian attack in Xinjiang region five months later, Chen was sent to a short-term labor assignment in Conghua, located north of Guangzhou. There, she helped the army build a watchtower on top of a mountain, part of a larger effort to construct a national system of shelters, tunnels, and lookouts. Chen carried cement and large rocks to the top of the mountain. The work was backbreaking, torturous, and long and continued for several weeks.

Without notice, in January 1970, two officials from the Guangzhou Beijing Opera Troupe summoned Chen to audition for concertmaster of the opera orchestra, which combined six to ten traditional Chinese instruments[21] and a Western double-wind orchestra with a small string section of seven to eight players, which Chen ultimately led. That same evening, an army review board was to review the troupe's performance of a model opera. One of the officials, a schoolmate from No. 29 Middle School, had remembered Chen's exceptional violin abilities and sought her out specifically for this opportunity. Chen auditioned with Sarasate's *Zigeunerweisen* and sight-read passages from the model opera *Taking Tiger Mountain by Strategy* (Edwards and Miller, 2020, p. 17). Thus began her work with the troupe that lasted for the next eight years (Figure 10).

---

[21] The traditional Chinese instruments included the *jinghu* and *jingerhu*, *yueqin*, *erhu*, *pipa*, *sanxian*, *yangqin*, and *ruan*.

For the first time, Chen was immersed in the intricacies and notations of Beijing opera and folk songs, which formed her knowledge of Chinese music and honed her skills as a musical and cultural translator. Her roommate during this period was *pipa* player Zhu Lei. Chen learned about *pipa* playing and the process of converting Western to cipher notation and vice versa as well as the right-hand fingerings notated on the top of the staff and left-hand ones on the bottom. Additionally, she learned how to play Chinese instruments such as the *ruan*.

As a result, she learned orchestration and performance practice for Western and traditional instruments, which gave her a head start once she entered conservatory. Members of the ensemble copied their own parts with Chen's assistance and singers brought scores in cipher notation that Chen read and transposed upon request. Also, there were a great number of orally transmitted musical conventions that Chen had to absorb as the leader of the hybrid orchestra. These included passages that accompanied martial scenes with cymbals (upbeat) and a drum (downbeat). Such hands-on experiences equipped Chen to navigate Western and Chinese musical practices with ease.

Figure 10 Chen Yi, concertmaster, Guangzhou Beijing Opera Orchestra, 1973. Chen Yun is behind her in the dark shirt. (photo courtesy of Chen Yi)

During this time, Chen also practiced the violin intensely (six hours a day) and worked on Western pieces, which were acceptable because they helped improve her technique for playing model works. She studied violin concertos by Beethoven, Paganini, Tchaikovsky, Brahms, Sibelius, Prokofiev, and J. S. Bach's Sonatas and Partitas, and other Western works with Zheng Rihua (Figure 11) and the legendary violin pedagogue Lin Yao Ji, the "father" of violin education in China.

Family members in Hong Kong – her Baptist missionary uncle and his pianist wife – also contributed to Chen's growth by sending music scores. Though officially prohibited, Chen acquired a certificate of permission from the Guangzhou Beijing Opera Troupe to receive these parcels from customs officials, a privilege she enjoyed as a professional musician in a government-approved performance group.

In addition, she absorbed the folk and revolutionary songs in the *yangbanxi* – the only officially approved melodies throughout China. The troupe performed ten to twenty times a month to a full house and at an extremely high level. Following every performance, there was dinner and a meeting to review all the mistakes and imperfections. Chen would indicate intonation problems and passages that weren't played correctly. The next morning, rehearsals were held to correct the problems and to practice scales. This was a period of stifling artistic conformity and control, and yet, it equipped Chen with a musical vocabulary and skills for her future compositions.

Figure 11 Chen Yi, Zheng Rihua, and Chen Yun, 1973 in Guangzhou
(photo courtesy of Chen Yi)

Over eight years, Chen played nearly all of the modernized Beijing operas and traveled to various locations in Guangdong Province to perform for audiences. The opera company also viewed exhibitions in Guangzhou by expert Beijing opera groups from the capital. Given the limited number of works performed throughout the country, the government eventually relaxed the restrictions and permitted regional opera companies to submit their own works for approval. Ideological purity, appropriateness of subject matter, and compositional quality were scrutinized. With Chen's participation, the Guangzhou Beijing Opera Troupe contributed a few original works. Chen composed overtures, incidental music, and orchestral interludes, orchestrated the aria accompaniments, and created arrangements for smaller ensembles of musicians who made excursions to the countryside. During these visits, Chen also learned to do the work of the local people, whether it be at shipping ports or on farms. It was thought that by assisting in this work, the musicians would better capture their comrades' emotions and sentiments as they performed the revolutionary works.

At Zengcheng, a district of Guangzhou, Chen developed deep friendships with a family of farmers. The father of the family traveled into the city to do menial work and his wife tended to the home and raised the children. In the early hours of the morning, Chen walked a long distance to gather dry wood used for cooking and to carry sizeable jugs of water from a well. She also learned how to cook using a large wok over a wood-fired stove. Chen "tasted the farmers' lives" and experienced "what they think, what they work for, and what is important to them." She gained a genuine connection with and respect for rural people.

Through these difficult experiences, Chen found her cultural roots, a new understanding of her mother country, and a profound appreciation for the working poor. "Frankly, it was not until then that I found my roots, my motherland, and really appreciated the simple people on the earth and the importance of education and civilization" (Edwards and Miller, 2020, p. 16). Her experiences also lent extra meaning to her father's words in reference to Mozart's music: "We played Mozart's music from childhood. [My father said], 'If you taste his music you'll feel happiness, you'll feel the brightness. But . . . you [don't] know that tears are running down his cheeks because you don't know his life.'" These experiences afforded Chen a glimpse into her rural countrymen's lives – their joys and struggles.

During this time, Chen and her brother also benefitted from additional academic instruction once she returned to Guangzhou. Since Chen had the ear to help her fellow musicians in the orchestra, Ge Wu, the orchestra conductor, suggested she study composition. For this purpose, Chen Ernan hired Zheng

Zhong to teach her and Chen Yun music theory. Every week, he systematically taught diatonic and chromatic harmony using the Sposobin and Walter Piston textbooks. Chen Yi also studied music history and theory articles translated by Liao Naixiong, a professor at the Shanghai Conservatory and *Modes and Harmony of the Han Nationality* by Li Yinghai. Other sources included Chinese translations of articles from the *Neue Zeitschrift für Musik* by Schumann and *Monsieur Croche – Antidilettante* by Debussy. In addition, Zheng Zhong lent her a book of folk songs. The songs were classified by province and ethnic minority group. She absorbed their styles, forms, and nuanced syllabic treatments. The naturalness of Chen's ethnic compositional voice began to emerge during this time. When Zheng heard one of the Beijing opera melodies she composed, he commented, "I love this. This is really from your voice, your heart, your mind . . . This is the most interesting music to come from you. As you have black eyes and black hair, your blood is Chinese . . . You drink water from the Yangtze River." (Chen later incorporated this melody in the *Fiddle Suite*, 3rd Movement.)

While home on Shamian Island one day, the head of the Chinese news agency informed Du that "higher education would reopen soon." Official word of this was announced in the newspapers, so Chen applied via the Guangzhou Beijing Opera Troupe upon receiving their permission. Chen was ranked the No. 1 candidate from Guangzhou. Owing to her compositional experience at the opera company and private instruction, she was well-prepared for formal training at the conservatory.

4.4 Central Conservatory (1978–1983)

Chen's improvisational abilities on the violin equipped her to experiment with composition while serving in the Guangzhou Beijing Opera Troupe's orchestra. By this time, her understanding of both Western music and *yangbanxi* was well established. Her studies with Zheng Zhong in both Western harmony and theory as well as Chinese folk songs advanced her academic preparedness, but new teachings in both Western modernism and Chinese folk idioms at the conservatory formed the underpinnings of her early modernism.

Initially, Chen applied to both the composition and violin departments at the Central Conservatory. She submitted three works that included overtures and incidental music she had written for the Guangzhou Beijing Opera Troupe and its string ensembles. Chen took three days of exams in music fundamentals, ear training, composition, and essay writing to qualify as a composition major. She also performed Paganini's *Caprice* No. 13 and the first movement of the Tchaikovsky Violin Concerto for the violin department jury. Because of her extensive performance and practice experience while in the Guangzhou Beijing Opera Troupe, Chen was able to play as many as ten major violin concertos in addition to some violin sonatas. Though admitted to both programs, Chen decided to major in composition and continued studying violin performance with Lin Yaoji on the side.

Beginning in the spring of 1978, Chen said that the students were "so hungry" to learn that they added this semester to the five-year bachelor's degree program, which officially started in the fall of 1978. Chen met students from all over the country who inspired her. For the first time, she was surrounded by musicians from outside of Guangzhou. These colleagues spoke other dialects in addition to Mandarin and Cantonese. They were also talented in art and writing. Chen referred to them as "real creators."

Initially, the ideology of the Cultural Revolution seeped into the Central Conservatory's reopening, with an ongoing prohibition of twentieth-century modernist or experimental works. Even Impressionism was criticized, as were the works of Shostakovich. Most of her studies were in tonal practice (Classical and Romantic periods) with courses in harmony (a review of the Sposobin textbook), counterpoint, four semesters of ear training, orchestration, piano instruction, and analysis. (Chen shared that Zhou Long had a head start in his education, having already studied many of these subjects before entering conservatory, and that counterpoint was not offered until she was a sophomore, but would have been helpful in her first-year compositions.) At first the ear training was "too easy," but it quickly progressed to four-part dictations at a very fast tempo. She placed at the top of her class in her academics and became one of the student leaders for the composition class as a result.

Required courses in art song also equipped her with a vast knowledge of Chinese indigenous music, a critical element in the development of her compositional style. The combined learning during her bachelor's and master's degree programs was rigorous and systematic. Chen stated:

> I began an eight-year, systematic study of Chinese traditional music ... The required courses of Chinese traditional music included Chinese folk songs (from all provinces and ethnic groups, in local dialects), traditional instrumental music (including plucking, bowing, blowing, and percussion instruments), local operas (history and the styles of singing, as well as reciting, acting, accompaniment, makeup, costume, stage setting, etc.), and narrative music (*Qu Yi*, which is musical storytelling that is half spoken and half sung) (Chen, 2002, p. 60).

Due to Zheng Zhong's efforts prior to conservatory, Chen possessed a basic knowledge of the folk song styles that existed but was not as familiar with the various dialects. Every week for two semesters, Chen memorized two stanzas from four songs and sang them in the proper dialect before a faculty group. In exams, students were asked to name the region and dialect of a song within a minute and compose one in a fixed form, rhyme scheme, and style with a given text from the Qing Dynasty. This eventually led to an important insight about the Chinese language, music, and nature: "I felt that if I were to create my music in a language with which I am most familiar, using logical principles that are related to nature, then my compositions would be very natural in emotion and powerful in spirit. This is my ideal" (Chen, 2002, p. 60).

Since she was less familiar with Chinese indigenous music, this learning provided a musical vocabulary and knowledge that anchored her cultural sensibility while providing structural principles for her music. Supplemental fieldwork trips to the countryside also reinforced her learning. The most memorable trip took place in the winter of 1981 to Guangxi Province, where the hosts sang and danced for their guests. Chen's first major piano work, *Duo Ye* (1984), composed during her master's degree, drew inspiration from this experience.

Chen's private composition teacher and mentor during her eight years of study at the Central Conservatory was Wu Zuqiang, an accomplished peda-gogue with a keen interest in form and analysis. Born to a family of traditional Chinese scholars, Wu studied at the Central Conservatory before the Communist takeover in 1949 and continued for another five years at the Moscow State Tchaikovsky Conservatory of Music. He then returned to China, composing orchestral works and ballets, ultimately settling at the Central Conservatory to establish a new composition program. He was fully steeped in the Western tradition of harmony, counterpoint, and orchestration and was supportive of Chen's compositional explorations. Chen described him as being "so open." At her lessons, she would share new material she had com-posed by playing it at the piano, a habit she continued at Columbia as a student of Chou Wen-Chung and Mario Davidovsky.

Studies with Wu also consisted of analyzing works by Tchaikovsky, Schumann, and Chopin. Chen said, "He would indicate how many variations and textures there are and how many subdivisions one could find belonging to the different keys. Variations could be grouped into larger sections ... and he would ask me to tell him all the forms of the Chopin Preludes, all twenty-four."

Chen's earliest composition at the conservatory was a set of piano preludes. She recalled bringing in four different beginnings to each prelude and Wu choosing one for each, while explaining his choice. He provided a critique about the sample beginnings such as "this doesn't have [an] obvious character," "this is too smooth," "this is too boring," or "it isn't refined enough." By the spring of 1979, Chen had composed two works: *Fisherman's Song* for violin and piano, with its ornamented pentatonic expression emulating Cantonese folk songs, and *Variations on* "Awaraguli" for piano, based on a Chinese folk song, "*Awariguli*," the name of a girl from the Uyghur (Turkic ethnic) minority in Xinjiang. The *Fisherman's Song* was an assigned work that was a complex three-part form and the *Variations on "Awariguli"* was a work inspired by Zhou's *Mongolian Folk-Tune Variations* for piano. Subsequent works from her undergraduate studies include the String Quartet (1982), a substantial composition in three movements that she later arranged for string orchestra as *Shuo* (1st movement) and *Sprout* (2nd movement). The String Quartet is a tonal work with a sonata-style first movement, a double canon in the second movement as inspired by the technique she learned in her counterpoint class (using the "*Jieshi*" Tune of *You Lan*), and a sonata-rondo statement for the finale using materials from the first two movements.

Wu stressed the importance of Bartók and his achievement of an Eastern and Western European musical synthesis in the six string quartets. Bartók's three levels of folk music integrations in the context of sophisticated classical structures served as a natural model for Chen and other "New Wave" modernists. She and her colleagues identified with Bartok's three-tiered approach to folk music integration: (1) a literal use of a folk melody with added accompaniment; (2) the stylistic imitation of a folk melody; and (3) the ability to compose freely in the folk spirit, having fully absorbed its style. Bartók's incorporation of folk music made logical sense to the Chinese, but musicologist Frank Kouwenhoven theorizes there may also be rhythmic, melodic, and harmonic relationships between Hungarian and Chinese folk music that "create natural affinities" (Kouwenhoven, 1992, p. 24).

Further into Chen's bachelor's degree program, the conservatory became more accepting of modernist expressions. Chen's soundscape opened up considerably with her exposures to Witold Lutoslawski and Alexander Goehr. Hearing Lutoslawski's Cello Concerto through classmate Hu Yongyan was transformational. She "jumped up suddenly" and said, "This is my voice," as the music's "fear and anger" resonated with her. Lutoslawski's modernism gave Chen an alternative to the Romantic style she was used to studying. Known for his absorption of Polish folk music as a mother tongue, Lutoslawski became the kind of modernist Chen wanted to be in his personalized use of twelve-tone techniques and ability to connect with the listener. Visits by the avant-garde composer Alexander Goehr in the spring of 1980 further equipped her to fulfill this aspiration.

Wu had befriended Goehr while judging a competition in London, which resulted in Goehr's repeated visits to China after the Cultural Revolution. Goehr, whose mentors included Schönberg and Messiaen, was the first

Western composer to visit China once it reopened and had a significant influence on Chen. In May and June 1980, Goehr had a three-week residency at the Central Conservatory where he gave ten lectures on twentieth-century composers and post-tonal techniques, worked with Chen and five other students (Ye Xiaogang, Zhou Qinru, Ge Gan-Ru, Wang Chengyong, and Lin Dehong), and held public masterclasses twice-weekly. Professors and students from all over China filled the classroom to watch as students presented their chamber works and received comments. Chen's first assignments were to compose a work for three string instruments as well as short songs based on a text by poet Li Po from the Tang Dynasty.

Goehr introduced atonality and covered twentieth-century works up to Messiaen, thus affording Chen her first significant exposure to twelve-tone techniques. Though an ardent serialist in the Darmstadt style during the 1960s, Goehr adopted a freer approach to the technique by the 1970s, at times incorporating tonal and modal elements (Griffiths, 1985, pp. 16–18). Responding to his encouragement to cultivate an original voice, the students turned to Chinese folk songs and incorporated dissonances rather than using the pentatonic mode or tonality. Goehr fixed pitches according to atonal techniques and voice leading rules and explained the conflict of dissonances and possible resolutions. Chen said, "He would talk naturally about your music and not based on a formula." The final assignment was a flute solo based on a favorite poem. Goehr instructed Chen to recite her Tang Dynasty poem numerous times to absorb the intonation and rhythm of the text before composing. Through these assignments, Goehr worked to cultivate each composer's voice and individuality.

Her graduation work, *Xian Shi* (1982), written for viola, piano, and percussion and later arranged for viola and orchestra as a concerto (1983), was the first Chinese viola concerto and marked a major advancement in Chen's personal voice. She incorporated the folk music modes and rhythms of *The Lions Play the Ball* from *Xianshi*, a popular instrumental ensemble music from Chaozhou, Guangdong Province. Chen describes the work as follows:

> You could tell then I was influenced by Lutoslawski, right? This piece is tonal [significant pentatonic presence], but both the form and the language are no longer pure. They are kind of a hybrid ... It could be considered as a sonata and also not a sonata because there is no strict recap. Instead, you have a big cadenza for the secondary material combined with the first material. This hybrid is influenced by twentieth-century language and music.

Throughout her training, Chen demonstrated a strong humanitarian impulse and desire to connect with people, much like her parents. Her compassion for her rural countrymen engendered during her farming assignments as a youth extended to her classmates at the conservatory. At the Central Conservatory, the electricity would go out at 11 pm, but the students would use flashlights to work under blankets. Students with no background in piano or composition had to work extra hard to catch up. At times, they found the workload overwhelming, so Chen assisted by playing their works so they could hear how they sounded and thus be improved.

Though competition for piano practice rooms was fierce, her natural gifts enabled her to "memorize the folk songs and even the fingerings for individual fugue voices in Bach's Well-Tempered Clavier" while lying on her bed. She was in this and every other regard a "model student."

4.5 Master's Degree Program at the Central Conservatory (1983–1986)

Unlike Zhou, who was employed by the China National Broadcasting Corporation upon completing his undergraduate degree, Chen continued her studies at the Central Conservatory as a master's candidate from 1983 to 1986. In the final years of her bachelor's degree program and during her master's program, China had become more open to modernist works. During these years, Chen began to experiment further. She asked, "what kind of language would fit my generation? Because we are not going to follow the old generation forever, we had to find a new language and new spirit as well."

More opportunities to learn from Western and Asian composers further expanded her outlook. German composer and pedagogue Dieter Acker visited to give a lecture and masterclass. Chen recalled his detailed chromatic analysis of Berg's Piano Sonata, Op.1. Also, Zhong Zilin, her professor in twentieth-century composition techniques, taught the six master's degree students the details of modern composition including post-tonal techniques. He also worked in the library and translated articles from English to Chinese, thus exposing the students to new scholarship in musicology and theory and to a growing LP and score collection of twentieth-century works including those of Chou Wen-Chung, Tōru Takemitsu, and Hans Werner Henze. An additional opportunity to attend an Isang Yun festival in Pyongyang, North Korea in 1985 gave Chen exposure to a Korean composer she deeply admired. For both Zhou and Chen, Isang Yun was an exemplar – a pioneering modernist who had not sacrificed his Korean cultural voice. For her master's thesis, Chen analyzed Isang Yun's work for orchestra entitled, *Muak* (1978).

Chen continued to produce works in two main areas: compositions that incorporated seed materials or principles from Chinese folk sources to create

Western-influenced modernist works and those that imitated the Chinese folk music style more overtly. One prominent example from the first category is *Duo Ye* (1984) for piano. Chen had visited the Guangxi Zhuang Autonomous Region of China where she witnessed the *Duo Ye* folk dance of the Dong minority villagers. She employed original musical material in the form of the syllabic rhythm and pitches for the opening "*Ya, Duo Ye*" that the group sings. Using register, she offset these statements antiphonally with the village leader's improvisational text and short tunes (Chen, 2002, p. 61). The work is a nonstandard or hybridized adaptation of sonata form that loosely explores twelve-tone procedures in the middle section along with a recitation of a Beijing opera tune and a twelve-note ostinato in the bass (Edwards and Miller, 2020, pp. 79–81). Her form and analysis professor, Yang Ruhuai, who oversaw fieldwork, encouraged the students to be inventive with traditional forms, hence its untraditional final section and coda, which bring together "all of the motives explored earlier, presenting them in new guises" (Edwards and Miller, 2020, p. 81). *Duo Ye* was originally titled *Sonata for Piano*, but Wu encouraged her to give it a more distinct, memorable name. A work in the second category is *Yu Diao* (1985), which she submitted for a piano pedagogical works competition. Here she sets a tonal Chinese melody in an ABA structure but uses a two-part invention texture in the B section as inspired by Hindemith's use of shifting rhythms and meter. Her piano work, *Small Beijing Gong* (1993), which is grouped with *Yu Diao* (1985) under the title *Two Bagatelles*, hints of the cross-cultural instrumental treatments Zhou Long explores, except without extended techniques. Here, Chen imitates the Beijing opera instrumental ensemble and singer but adds a Western modernist feature with dissonant intervals, a seven-note ostinato figure, and frequent metric changes.

In her final months at the Central Conservatory, Chen varied her explorations further. She composed *Two Sets of Wind and Percussion Instruments* (1986), which reflects Varèse's influence with its sound effects. Conductor Shui Lan encouraged her to consider an antiphonal approach to the work, with two ensembles responding to each other from opposite locations on the stage. In Symphony No. 1 (1986), her master's graduation composition, atonal dissonances come to the fore, which she attributes to Bartok's Concerto for Orchestra, a work she analyzed in her orchestration class. A single-movement work in three parts, Chen features a retrograde double fugue and unison textures in the first part, a scherzo-like second part, and solos for unheralded instruments such as the English horn, saxophone, and viola in the final part – a metaphor for the importance of all voices (Chen, 1986). The culmination of her master's degree program was a concert of her orchestral works from 1986 including *Two Sets of Wind and Percussion Instruments*, *Duo Ye* (chamber orchestra version), *Xian Shi* (Viola Concerto), *Sprout* (for string orchestra), and Symphony No. 1.

Though Chen's formal academic exposure to modernism was formative, the more critical discovery was her natural attraction to atonality, an organic outgrowth from the way she hears speech. During her field trips to gather folk tunes from farmers and villagers, Chen discovered that she hears pitches when people speak. Thus, she could translate poetry recitations or speech into musical pitches, which helped with the transcriptions she created. When transcribing folk songs, she would use arrows to mark the pitch up or down to capture the microtonal inflections in their speech. Her unique aural association of speech to pitch is apparent in *Three Poems from the Song Dynasty* (1985) for mixed chorus with solos for soprano, alto, and tenor. This was Chen's first choral work. An original a cappella piece, all three movements exhibit a lyrical, melodic treatment as opposed to a chorale or syllabic texture. The first movement is a setting of a poem by Li Qingzhao with aleatoric treatment, the second movement is a recitation of text by Xin Qiji with pitches (Chen later uses this "speech song" technique in her pitch writing for instrumental playing), and the third movement is based on text by Su Shi with polyphonic settings and unison singing.

In her Chinese instrumental class, Professor Yuan Jingfang analyzed the music of Chinese traditional instrumental ensembles. Yuan, a scholar in the field of ethnomusicology, published a book dedicated to traditional percussion ensemble music with her own classification system including *yu he ba* (patterns with the sum of eight), which Chen used in *Xian Shi* and *Duo Ye*. She employs an antiphonal dialogue where individual rhythmic parts contract and expand inversely in response to the other as found in *Shifan luogu*, a type of percussion ensemble music in southeastern China. Chen describes this as "a telescopic principle ... [in which] the combinations and contrasts between high and low parts, the design of the meters, and the numbers of groupings of notes, are all inspired by the original rhythmic organizations called 'The Sum of Eight'" (Chen, 2002, p. 61). This technique organizes notes between two instruments or groups according to the following pattern: 7+1, 5+3, 3+5, 1+7. Chen also uses the "Golden Olive" pattern where rhythmic groupings are patterned palindromically: 1, 3, 5, 7, 5, 3, 1 (Chen, 2002, p. 63).

Other sources of inspiration included new music recordings and recording opportunities. Zhou's resident composer status at the China National Broadcasting Symphony provided access to the radio library and recording studio, so Central Conservatory students orchestrated their art songs and Chen had her own works performed. *Xie Zi* (1985) for Chinese traditional ensemble (*liuqin, pipa, sanxian, sheng, bangdi, zhudi,* and percussion) was one such work. It was later performed by Music From China in 1991, once Chen was studying at Columbia.

Through the generosity of Chen's uncle in Hong Kong, she received a Yamaha DX-7 synthesizer and developed basic fluency with electronic music. Zhou and Chen participated in the first electronic music group at the conservatory, inspired by French pop and electronic composer Jean-Michel Jarre's visit. Just prior to Zhou's departure for America, they held the first concert of electronic music in China (1985) that included their works and those of other master's degree students – Tan Dun, Chen Yuanlin, and Zhu Shirui. As early as 1986, Chen began experimenting with electronic music in her Symphony No. 1, where she incorporated a synthesized sound of a large gong. At Columbia, she continued these studies with Mario Davidovsky and with Pril Smily who taught electronic music history and basic techniques.

In 1986, Chen graduated from the Central Conservatory, the first female to earn a master's degree in composition, and left for the United States to join Zhou at Columbia.[22] Chen said she felt academically equipped and emotionally prepared for the cultural transition.

4.6 Doctoral Program at Columbia (1986–1993)

Chen's works at Columbia University demonstrate a sophisticated and varied use of modernist techniques. The foundation in modernism provided during her bachelor's program, under the influence of Goehr and Lutoslawski, followed by additional systematic studies of twentieth-century techniques during her master's degree program, culminated in an array of experimentations while at Columbia University. Serialism and Chinese number theories rose to the fore in her final works from this period.

Like Zhou and the other Chinese students who entered the DMA program around the same time, Chen studied with Chou Wen-Chung, who transmitted Chinese cultural resources through philosophy and aesthetics, while encouraging avant-garde explorations. Chou spurred Chen and others to revive the work of the *wenren* – ancient artist-philosophers – by drawing upon the rich repository of Chinese cultural and artistic expressions. By doing so, this new generation of composers would "contribute meaningfully and on equal terms with the West towards a true *confluence* of musical cultures" (Chou, 2007, p. 501).

By 1987, Chen also had opportunities to learn from Mario Davidovsky, who taught a required electronic music class, and George Edwards in twentieth-

---

[22] Chen and Zhou fully expected to return to China once their DMA degrees were completed.

Figure 12 Chen Yi, Chou Wen-Chung, George Edwards, and Zhou Long, 2001
(photo courtesy of Zhou Long)

century theory (Figure 12). Although she had learned about and experimented
with twelve-tone techniques at the Central Conservatory, the Woodwind
Quintet (1987) exhibits Chen's most extensive incorporation of serial techniques, though used in a free manner. In the opening section, she employs
a twelve-tone row and its fragments and separates them with rests so the players
can take a breath. Cast in a polyphonic texture, these rests become inaudible as
the texture thickens and a polyrhythmic interplay of voices ensues. The middle
section, which is not serial, presents a melody with tone clusters, inspired by
a visit to Putuo Mountain in Zhejiang Province where she heard Buddhist nuns
chanting at a temple. The singing was not in unison, so Chen cast this sound
phenomenon heterophonically. As is typical for Chen, the recapitulation is
replaced with a final section that combines materials from the opening and
middle sections but presented in different forms (Edwards and Miller, 2020,
p. 83). Though instructionally guided by Chou, the work was premiered in 1987
at the 42nd Annual Composers' Conference at Wellesley College under
Davidovsky's direction.

Chen also arranged *Duo Ye* (1984), originally composed for solo piano and
arranged for chamber orchestra in 1985, for full orchestra in 1987. For a fuller,
more idiomatic use of a triple-wind orchestra with percussion, Chen added an
introduction and changed the middle section to substitute for the contrapuntal
writing in the piano version. These changes were substantial enough to warrant
a new title, *Duo Ye No. 2* (1987). A Stravinskyan quality is present in the
orchestral version with its frequent meter changes and polytonality.

Other atonal works from this period include *Near Distance* (1988), a sextet
for flute, clarinet, violin, cello, piano, and percussion. It is a fully atonal but
nonserial work that Chen wrote to qualify for the Aspen Festival with Jacob
Druckman's encouragement. It incorporates an imitation of white noise at the
conclusion as the instrumentalists create a continuous "sss" sound with their
mouths. Chen identifies this work as being her "most personal" (Zheng, 2010,
pp. 258–259) and makes the connection between Chinese speech patterns and
"gestures" in Chinese instrumental performance: "Yet, music played ... with
that phrasing, that rise and fall [of the sound], would give a special feeling, more
similar to Chinese language. There is atonal technique in this piece ... but those
detailed gestures were extracted from the performance practice of Chinese
instruments" (Zheng, 2010, p. 259). Another atonal work, *As in a Dream*
(1988), two songs for soprano, violin, and cello (arranged for soprano, pipa,
zheng, 1994; soprano and zheng, 2010), is a serial work where Chen adopts
a singing technique reminiscent of *Sprechstimme*. Chen learned about
Sprechstimme from Zhong Zilin and was instantly drawn to it since it "match-
[ed] her aesthetic" and captured the pitch associations she hears in spoken
Chinese with its tonal inflections. The work also displays the recitation style
of Beijing opera along with free atonal techniques. Imitations of Chinese
plucked instruments through extended techniques on string instruments also
abound to accompany the voice texture. Particularly noteworthy is the idiomatic
writing in the voice part. With the guidance of singer Rao Lan, Chen learned
how to use the high register effectively even in soft dynamics and to extract the
full resonance of the chest voice in the low register. Finally, *Monologue—
Impressions on "The True Story of Ah Q"* for solo clarinet (1993), is
a dramatic free atonal work based on a novel with the same title by political
satirist Lu Xun.

A commission from the Renee B. Fisher Awards Competition for pianists
aged 14–18 inspired *Guessing* (1989), a solo piano work with a set of variations
on an "antiphonal folk song" cast in a free atonal style with quartal and quintal
harmonies, polymodal counterpoint, and Stravinskyan rhythms. A variety of
textures that are polyphonic, lyrical, chordal, and percussive test the pianist's
control of the pedal, voicing, articulations, and dynamics.

Even as Chen composed for Western instruments, she also composed for
Chinese traditional instruments, a practice she acquired while at the Central
Conservatory, which required one work of this type annually. *The Tide* (1988),
a septet for *xun, yangqin, pipa, zheng, gaohu, erhu,* and percussion, which was
composed for Music From China, exhibits a free atonality without motivic
development. The Overture No. 1 (1989) and Overture No. 2 (1990) for
Hong Kong Chinese Orchestra are examples of her interest in ancient court

music with its layered approach to instrumental sections and sound texture. She explained that her extensive training in both Western and Chinese music at the Central Conservatory made it very easy to cross over from one idiom to the next. Commissioned by the New York New Music Consort for *pipa* player Wu Man in 1991, Chen composed *The Points* for *pipa*, which became a popular work for international Chinese traditional instrument competitions. In 1992, Chen adopted *The Points* as the first movement and added two more movements that same year to create an ensemble version entitled the *Suite*, a quintet for *pipa, dizi, yangqin, sanxian,* and *erhu.* She remarked that writing for Wu Man informed the texture of the work with all its virtuosic possibilities. The pipa has a wide range and more than seventy technical practices that include "tremolo, vibrato, glissando, pitch inflection, and harmonics" (Chen, 2002, p. 64). In preparation, Chen researched the *pipa* repertoire, both the lyrical and martial styles, absorbed the fingering techniques, and listened to the styles of *pipa* playing (Chen, 2002, p. 64). For imagery, Chen used the eight brushstrokes of the *yong* ("eternal") Chinese character in *Zhengkai* calligraphy to inform its structure. The title refers to the contact points between brush and paper – where a stroke begins and ends as well as the shape, "unique touch," and character of the eight strokes (Chen, 2002, p. 64). Chen also composed *Pipa Rhyme* (1992) for *pipa* master Tang Liangxing and the Taipei Municipal Chinese Classical Orchestra.

In 1991, Chou retired from Columbia and Davidovsky became Chen's dissertation advisor (Figure 13). His objective, logic-driven approach to structure resonated with her. As a capstone summation of her final two years at Columbia, Chen composed several works she refers to as being "academic" for their use of a twelve-tone row and the Golden Mean. These include *Sparkle* (1992), an octet for flute, clarinet, violin, cello, double bass, two percussionists, and piano, the Piano Concerto (1992), Symphony No. 2 (1993), and *Song in Winter* (1993), a trio for *dizi, zheng,* and harpsichord (arranged for flute, *zheng,* piano, and percussion in 1993 and later soprano, *zheng,* and piano in 2004). Chen also used Chinese folk elements that serve explicitly structural purposes, knowing that proportions in nature have resonance with human feeling and thought.

She related:

> For example, I found a Chinese folk tune *"Ba Ban"* (eight beats) that has more than 300 variations … [It] has a golden section, and also the grouping method follows the numbers of the Fibonacci series … If you see the human body, you see a ratio, proportion, .618, the ratio between the upper and lower parts of the body. If you look at flower petals or honeycomb made by bees, you see it's the same … It's nature! (Borger, 1999, pp. 278–280)

Figure 13 Chen Yi and Mario Davidovsky, 1987 (photo courtesy of Chen Yi)

She also states, "In the Chinese tradition" ... the number eight "symbolizes good fortune—which indicates the number of the most famous mountains, the directions of the compass, the divisions of the agricultural seasons in the lunar calendar, the principal syndromes in traditional medicine ... and so on" (Chen, 2002, p. 67). *Sparkle* (1992) incorporates the Golden Mean or Fibonacci Series relationships found in the Chinese folk tune *Baban*. The original Chinese *Baban* tune has eight phrases with eight quarter notes each. The one exception is the fifth phrase where four quarter notes are added at the end of the phrase (Chen, 2002, p. 66). In this sequence of eight phrases, the Golden Mean occurs precisely after five of the phrases (right before these four added notes) and before the final three phrases. Chen references the presence of the ratio of 5:3 (4.83:3 to be exact) in the natural world and the transference of this "natural feeling of balance from the visual arts and natural sciences to the form and rhythm of the music" (Chen, 2002, p. 67). The imagery of sparks – "everlasting flashes of wit, so bright, nimble, and passionate" – inspires the perpetual motion (Chen, 2002, p. 68). Cast in a ternary form, one hears the pentatonic *Baban* tune along with a twelve-tone row "integrated with each other horizontally and vertically throughout" (Chen, 2002, p. 68). In the Piano Concerto (1982), the *Baban* melody, rhythms, and proportions also figure significantly, governing even the lengths of the sections (Edwards and Miller, 2020, p. 68).[23]

---

[23] Chen Yi submitted the Piano Concerto along with an analysis of it to fulfill her DMA degree requirements.

Song in Winter (1993), an exceptional work in Chen's oeuvre for its mixed instrumentation, incorporates a twelve-tone row to mark significant structural moments, *Baban*, and *Shifan luogu* mathematical patterns (1, 2, 3, 5, 3, 2, 1) to control pitch groupings (Edwards and Miller, 2020, p. 85).

Finally, in Symphony No. 2 (1993), Chen opens the work in the low register with the same twelve-tone row she used in the Piano Concerto, *Sparkle*, and *Song in Winter* and a special motif (A, B, C, F, A-flat) that came to her when she learned her father had suffered a heart attack (Borger, 1999, p. 282). This work is a threnody for her father who passed away three years prior. In Chen's words:

> I hear the tragic motif of my symphony again and again, and I can't stop a tear from running down my cheek. That motif has been haunting me since I first learned my dear father had a heart attack. .... He led me into the realm of music when I was only three and helped me understand the sincerity and simplicity of Mozart (Edwards and Miller, 2020, pp. 60, 62).

Here, Chen's creativity reflects a philosophy akin to musical transnationalism – deeply emotional music that is born of highly structured elements that speak to listeners regardless of their culture. In Symphony No. 2, the twelve-tone row contains the dissonance of tritones and semitones to express her grief. It concludes with a reiteration of a Buddhist chant using these same intervals that builds to a climax as "the brass cries out in clusters FATHER or BABA" (Edwards and Miller, 2020, p. 62). Rhythmic topoi from Beijing opera's *luogu dianzi* are used to increase the intensity of the expression along the way.[24]

Much attention has been devoted to musical features in Chen's music that are distinctly Chinese and those that are Western or modern. Even more compelling, however, is Chen's use of themes and integrations that are deeply human and speak to listeners from different cultural backgrounds. Her education at Columbia gave her the insights and tools to do this through music. She explained:

> These courses gave me the ability to consider music not as a new versus historical, nor as Eastern versus Western, but rather to consider the fact that human thought goes into all of these musics. I began to see similarities in musical styles, aesthetics, customs, feelings, and principles. As I considered composing in my own unique language, in my most natural voice and style, I began to be inspired by what I had learned from various cultural traditions, and even from scientific principles. (Chen, 2002, pp. 63–64)

Though Symphony No. 2 is an expression of Chen's grief, it also pays tribute to Chen Ernan, his devotion to the Chinese people and general humanitarian

---

[24] The Beijing opera's percussion ensemble plays from 100 preexisting rhythmic patterns called *luogu dianzi* that possess dramatic meaning (Rao, 2007, p. 511).

aspirations. In the final measures, what was "a voice of yearning for civilization" floats away with a "dream forward to the future" (Chen, 1993).

5 Synthesis

The previous sections shed light on the opportunities, contingencies, and natural
proclivities that shaped Zhou and Chen's modernisms despite the Cultural
Revolution's dominating influence and narrative. Though they came of age
during the most repressive social, political, and cultural time in Chinese history
and attended the same institutions of higher learning, their styles diverged. How
does one account for this?

The differences can perhaps be explained by the external and internal factors
that played key roles in Zhou and Chen's growth as modernist composers.[25] The
early stages of their development present important external factors, that is,
circumstances over which they had no control, and the later stages highlight
internal ones – where personal choice or agency found expression. By examining these factors during these stages of formation, a framework for understanding Chen and Zhou as highly individual modernists emerges despite their shared
experiences of the Cultural Revolution and educations at the Central
Conservatory and Columbia University.

5.1 Shared and Divergent External Factors: Family History, Early Childhood Experiences, and Labor Assignments

" . . . the things I am most familiar with are the things most natural . . . " -Chen Yi

Both Zhou and Chen came from privileged families that had a profound appreciation for the arts and access to personal mentors. They viewed music education as the means to a future. The impact of this factor cannot be overstated, as
both families played a critical role in facilitating Zhou and Chen's education
before and during the Cultural Revolution.

Although the West is tempted to see the success of Zhou and Chen as natural
outcomes of their interests and talent, the interviews made it clear that the
Cultural Revolution played a role in making them composers. The eradication
of formal education, including schools of medicine and engineering, steered
Zhou and Chen toward disciplines where one-on-one instruction was possible.
In Zhou's words, "You can't study engineering by yourself, you have to attend
university, but there was no choice." As a result, Zhou studied music, poetry,
English, and literature – all autodidactic pursuits. Were it not for the Cultural

---

[25] Exploring the fluid interaction of nature and nurture is complex and beyond the scope of this
Element.

Revolution, Zhou would have pursued mechanical engineering. His middle school and life-long friend Gu Yan, a toxicologist at the US Food and Drug Administration, attested that both he and Zhou had ambitions of becoming engineers. He shared, "to be honest with you, I never thought he would become a composer." Chen's parents also had hopes that she and her siblings would train to become physicians. With all manner of formal education closed, however, both sets of parents resorted to homeschooling and found colleagues and resources to sustain this private study. This move proved crucial to their musical success. Chen enjoyed violin and music theory and history training through her teachers, Zheng Rihua and Zheng Zhong, for nearly two decades. Zhou, too, had music tutors in harmony, theory, orchestration, counterpoint, and songwriting from the China Conservatory and the Central Philharmonic in Beijing, prior to entering the Central Conservatory. Moreover, both listened to Western classical music through recordings and other sources, made possible through Chen Ernan's recording collection and access to live performances and Zhou's mother, He Gaoyong, and Aunt Zhu Min, who worked in Moscow. Lastly, both Zhou and Chen had parents who shaped their musical aspirations. Chen Ernan (Chen's father) and He Gaoyong (Zhou's mother) expressed their strong desires for their children to one day become "creators" of music.

Both also benefitted from unforeseen events that led to immersive musical work experiences during the Cultural Revolution. For Zhou, a back injury resulted in his transfer to Zhangjiakou. With the intervening help of his family friend, Li Xin, the son of Li Ling, an assignment with the Zhangjiakou Song and Dance Troupe followed that led to his work as an arranger and composer. Similarly, while Chen was laboring in the Shimen district, she was summoned to audition for the concertmaster position at the Guangzhou Beijing Opera Troupe orchestra. This role developed her fluency with Beijing opera and provided opportunities to compose short works (overtures and incidental music) for the troupe. The works Zhou and Chen composed in these settings enabled them to apply to and become part of the select cohort that was admitted to the Central Conservatory of Music in 1977.

Though both composers benefitted from these supportive family backgrounds, there were significant differences in their cultural exposures and identity formations. Chen's family was steeped in Western culture by virtue of her parents' profession, avocational interest in music, and location on Shamian Island, home to diplomats from around the world. Her family was fluent in English and engaged cross-culturally through literature, language (English, German, and Japanese), and current events. Her music training and listening, however, was completely Eurocentric. Chen states, "the things I am most familiar with are the things most natural" (Zheng, 2010, p. 257). Though she made this statement about Chinese language and culture, it applies equally to her musical sensibilities. Western classical music was ingrained not only in her mind but in her fingers, nervous system, and muscles. As a result, when she first tried to compose, the music sounded "Westernized" because her "training from three years old was Mozart." Chen had almost no exposure to Chinese indigenous music until the Cultural Revolution. The reeducation period on farms and later as a member of the Guangzhou Beijing Opera Troupe fostered a profound respect for the lifestyles, humility, and values of the working poor and anchored her Chinese cultural identity. She recalled:

> Frankly, it was not until then that I found my roots, my motherland, and really appreciated the simple people on the earth and the importance of education and civilization. I learned to overcome hardship, to bear anger, fear and humiliation under the political pressure, to get close to uneducated farmers on a personal and spiritual level, and to share my feelings and thinking with them . . . and to work hard in order to benefit more human beings in society. (Edwards and Miller, 2020, p. 16)

By contrast, Zhou's artistic and musical exposures at home were bicultural and interdisciplinary. His mother was a Western-trained opera professor and his father a set design artist. Together, they immersed Zhou in Western romantic opera arias, Chinese drama, literature, and art while living at the dormitory of The Central Academy of Drama. He also developed a keen ear for melody and vocal intonation because of his mother's voice instruction at home. Tang Dynasty poetry and indigenous Chinese music added to his sonic experiences. Particularly noteworthy is Zhou's strong preference for Chinese classical sources, which were banned during the Cultural Revolution. He delights in reconnecting with China's ancient sources, a likely influence of his mother. His Pulitzer Prize–winning opera *Madame White Snake*, for example, has Puccini-like arias and children's choir interludes that employ four Tang poems – remembrances of his childhood. As a result of his upbringing, Zhou's interest in music has always been interdisciplinary in nature and informed by abstract connections between different forms of expression – Western and Eastern, traditional and experimental, old and new, written and heard.

Despite this rich background, Zhou lacked the breadth of exposures to the West that Chen had while growing up. When Chen arrived in the United States, she felt completely at home, while Zhou suffered from "culture shock" and "homesickness." Lacking English fluency was his central challenge. According to Zhou, when he went to get his visa, "he couldn't produce a TOEFL score, nor converse." He tried to read English and "it went very badly." Because of this language issue, Professor Chou sent a telegram to the embassy and one to Zhou at the Conservatory along the lines of: "Please give Zhou Long, our doctoral candidate, a visa as soon as possible. He will be required to take an exam for English proficiency upon his arrival at Columbia." The impact of this language challenge was significant and affected his music-making, which is addressed in the next section.

Zhou and Chen's divergent experiences during the Cultural Revolution were also due to considerable differences in their family backgrounds. Though both were subject to hard labor, they were sent to very different geographic contexts, which influenced their musical growth. Zhou was assigned to Heilongjiang in northeast China near the Soviet border because of his paternal grandfather's *di* status, whereas Chen stayed in Guangdong Province, because her parents were intellectuals, *you*. Zhou's music learning and exposure in Heilongjiang was nonexistent for three years given its remote rural location, whereas Chen benefitted from remaining near Guangzhou, a major urban center.

Chen's ability to learn and practice the violin during the Cultural Revolution was deeply formative. While serving as concertmaster of the Guangzhou Beijing Opera Troupe, Chen found more time to practice her Western violin repertoire. Ironically, as soon as she was "internal" to the organization, this activity was protected. Chen states:

> In the Beijing Opera, I had more time to practice, because for professional musicians, you are allowed to study Western repertoire. It's not blocked anymore because it's internal. It's like you are protected because you are one of the members of the orchestra serving in the modern Beijing Opera group, right? And you are allowed to improve your technique. . . . I gave half of my practice time to [violin] practice, sometimes six hours a day on my Western repertoire.

The singular greatest difference during this early phase of their development was the way Chen and Zhou developed their musicianship. Chen developed hers by playing the violin and piano at a very high level. There is a unique musical fluency that is gained when the fingers and ears are highly trained from a young age. She also had absolute pitch, which informed much of her success in her formal education, not to mention the way that she hears and processes music. Zhou, by contrast, did not have a prodigious talent for an instrument. His musicality, which began with some exposure to the piano, was fed primarily by listening to his mother's voice lessons, recordings, and playing the accordion. In his teen years, he also enjoyed one-on-one instruction in harmony, theory, counterpoint, orchestration, and conducting. From this foundation grew his visionary musical ideas about cross-cultural instrumentation.

Historically speaking, two major categories of composers exist: those who began as instrumental prodigies and those who did not. For those who are prodigies, like Mozart and Beethoven, the aural and digital mastery of music leads to formal mastery. In *The Lives of the Great Composers*, Harold Schonberg writes:

> Child prodigies, instinct in music from babyhood, develop a certain kind of aural and digital response, and before they arrive at their teens they already are masters of technique. They have imbibed the literature from the cradle, have physically grappled with it, have become secure craftsmen, can do anything they want to do as easily as breathing. As they mature, they go as far as their imaginations allow, but always they develop into masters of form. They grow up automatically handling with finesse the *materials* of music (Schonberg, 1997, p. 152).

Continuing, he observes that composers like Wagner, and one might add Berlioz, who did not have an impressive instrumental talent, demonstrate a vision for the music that may be shaped more by "instinct and profound musicality" (Schonberg, 1997, p. 269). This musicality is also one tied to extramusical associations, often literary or visual. If one adopts Schonberg's view, Chen's technical fluency at the violin prepared her well, but not exclusively, for mastery of form or absolute music, and Zhou's honed instincts apart from instrumental mastery yielded compositions inspired by extra-musical imagery.

5.2 Divergent Internal Factors: The Central Conservatory, Postbaccalaureate, and Columbia Years

"The music is really attached to your personality. You can't change it." -Zhou Long

These two contingencies certainly apply to Zhou and Chen; however, the most profound differences in their modernisms are rooted in their personalities and wiring. Conductor JoAnn Falletta and students Wang Amao and Xi Wang described them as the perfect pairing of opposites. Pianist and niece Liang Xiaomin elaborated on this contrast through their piano pieces *Wu Kui* (Zhou) and *Duo Ye* (Chen): "Both are pretty virtuosic works, hard pieces. *Wu Kui* seems very natural to our technique, like how our fingers work. *Duo Ye* . . . you have to practice a lot more to make it work."

There is much to uncover in these comments. Zhou is a quiet introvert, Chen, an energetic extrovert. He writes more slowly, she composes quickly. He is philosophical; she is concrete. He enjoys big picture concepts; she revels in the details. He composes through abstract association; she, by sketching out form, ideas, and structure. She enjoys academic work and analyzing music; he, much less so. Zhou noted, "The music is really attached to your personality. You can't change it. If you really want to change it, it's fake. It's not really organic." Zhou's point is an important one – personality, which drives choices, is something one inherits and is the central reason for their divergent modernisms. Both composers learned the same curriculum at the Central Conservatory and Columbia University and were exposed to the same influences. So, which Western influences prevailed in cultivating their individual modernisms? For Zhou, Chou and Varèse figured significantly and for Chen, Lutoslawski, Goehr, and Davidovsky, which speak to their unique natures.

Zhou's epiphanies or moments of enlightenment (he frequently uses the phrase "opened up my mind") reflect a tendency toward philosophical thinking and solitude combined with a love for Chinese classical aesthetics. This quality in combination with Su Xia's systematic teaching prepared Zhou to pursue a pioneering yet holistic modernism. Rather than choosing Western compositional techniques as the primary route, Zhou chose instead to build new "sound fields" that connect East and West, old and new. This was in keeping with Chou's injuncture that Chinese composers familiarize themselves with their cultural (literary, visual, musical, and philosophical) past.

These encouragements had significant creative implications. By their very nature, Chinese folk music, opera, and *guqin* music resist analytical studies because they are largely improvised and emphasize process rather than notation and structure. Chinese scholar Jiti Li writes, "In the traditional Chinese concept, music is the presentation of 'process' and 'mood,' and the key to appreciating it is to not focus on musical form and structure, but to concentrate on its feelings and understand the flowing process of the music and overall mood" (Li, 2004, p. 6). This aligned well with Chou's interdisciplinary way of thinking and Zhou's.

In *Polycultural Synthesis in the Music of Chou Wen-Chung*, Zhou describes the holistic nature of his creativity: "The way I compose is actually very similar to Professor Chou's. Images of poetry and painting provide inspiration for the music itself – not just for the collections of sounds, but also for the concepts" (Arlin and Radice, 2018, p. 260). Rather than describing compositional techniques, he speaks of big picture concepts and the feelings they evoke. In our conversations about compositional process, Zhou referenced *The Man of Iron and the Golden Spike*, his oratorio based on the Chinese railroad workers who built the Pacific railroad in the West, and other mature works as they relate to extramusical association:

> I enjoyed working on the story and visiting the site and the museum to collect materials and the folk poems from Canton, the workers' hometown. I also enjoyed the opera [*Madame White Snake*] for the legend ... I have some instrumental works, but they are always inspired by the poems from the Tang Dynasty.... With the exception of *Mongolian Folk-Tune Variations*, which

is based on a folk tune, almost everything has a title or some story that is from a painting or literature. I think that's what I enjoy composing the most. It is different from ... composing a Sonata Opus 1, No. 1.

This philosophical or extramusical approach informed Zhou's early innovations of adapting Eastern instrumental performance practices to Western instruments, a practice he explored throughout the scope of this study (1953–93). These explorations were possible because of his considerable knowledge about orchestration through private studies with Luo Zhongrong and his work experiences at Zhangjiakou and at the China National Broadcasting Corporation. In fact, his earliest ideas about cross-cultural instrumentation surfaced while at Zhangjiakou (1973–7), where he worked with both traditional and Western instruments. During his conservatory years, Chou's cross-cultural instrumental approach in works such as *Yü Ko* influenced Zhou's aesthetic, as seen in *Fisherman's Song* for orchestra (1981) and later in his *Song of the Ch'in* for string quartet (1982), one of his most recognized works.

By contrast, Chen, the extrovert, combines academic and performance expertise to connect across cultures. Her parents lived purposefully, animated by a genuine care for others. Their work included establishing hospitals, practicing medicine, and translating medical articles from English to Chinese. Chen followed suit. She helped classmates struggling with their studies, served as a representative in the Beijing municipal government while at the Central Conservatory, translated documents from English to Chinese for Chou Wen-Chung as his assistant at the Center for US-China Arts Exchange, taught classes as a teaching assistant at Columbia, and, once in America, became a musical ambassador through Music From China. Motivating it all was her love for people and an infectious optimism, a quality that animates her music.

Though primarily versed in tonal music as a violinist and pianist, her understanding of Western modernism and Chinese indigenous music evolved in parallel at the Central Conservatory. Like Zhou, she composed for both Western and traditional Chinese ensembles; however, she rarely mixed the two before 1993. The one exception for the scope of this study is *Song in Winter* (1993). Drawing from a wide range of Chinese cultural inspirations, Chen incorporated or drew inspiration from folk songs and dance, ancient poems from the Tang and Song dynasties, Peking opera, theater, Buddhist chants, and calligraphy among others with a consistent focus on structural innovation.

Consistent with Schonberg's insight, Chen valued formal integrity and analyzable details in her works and, with rare exceptions (e.g., *The Points*, 1991), composed music with structure rather than imagery in mind. Unlike Zhou, she composed absolute works, such as the String Quartet, Woodwind Quintet,

Symphony No. 1, Symphony No. 2, and Piano Concerto. Works with extra-musical titles like *Variations on "Awariguli"* for piano, *Xian Shi*, a viola concerto, and *Near Distance*, a sextet, also balance out the list from this period. Nevertheless, her emphasis on form remained consistent. She described *Xian Shi* in the following manner:

> This piece is tonal [significant pentatonic presence], but both the form and the language are no longer pure. They are kind of a hybrid, and they cross the border a little bit. It could be considered as a sonata and also not a sonata because there is no strict recap. Instead, you have a big cadenza for the secondary material combined with the first material. This hybrid is influenced by twentieth-century language and music.

Chen's music wed her Chinese cultural identity, which blossomed during the Cultural Revolution, with her theoretical studies in Western and Eastern music at the conservatory. Always a dedicated student, she searched for an authentic way of integrating her Chinese melodies and motifs with Western compositional techniques. This perspective evolved gradually with the influence of notable twentieth-century pedagogues. Chou's philosophical appeals to China's cultural past, Goehr's masterclasses on post-tonal techniques, Wu's structural analyses, and Lutoslawski's expressive sonic imagination shaped her perspective. But so did the theoretical analyses of Chinese instrumental music taught by Yuan Jingfang, a folk song class with Geng Shenglian and Zhao Songguang, music storytelling with Zhang Hongyi, traditional theater music with Luo Yinghui, and folk music field work in Guangxi Province and other locations. She also discovered the close connection between Chinese spoken language and music that made atonality attractive and offered insights into how she could achieve an authentic cultural synthesis:

> Because I believe that language can be translated into music, and because I speak naturally in my mother tongue, there are Chinese blood, Chinese philosophy, and Chinese customs in my music. However, because music is a universal language, I hope to capture the essence of both Eastern and Western cultures. (Roche Commissions, 2005, p. 69)

Rather than drawing upon linguistic and structural associations, Zhou turned to the classical *guqin* tradition for its cultural significance in Chinese history, its literary allusions and richness, and absence of rhythmic notation, which yields interpretive freedom. He stated, "I'm not good with pitches. Chen Yi is very good with pitches, but I am very interested in rhythms." The simple meters (2/4 and 4/4) and rhythms of Chinese folk songs didn't offer the same opportunities. His challenge, therefore, was to find a third way between the confines of simple meter in Chinese folk music and the unnotated liberties of the *guqin* tradition. In

Song of Ch'in (1982), he translated improvised *guqin* practices for string quartet by notating every metric and rhythmic detail, an effort that fueled his imagination. These explorations toward rhythmic freedom reached a high point in *Wuji* (1987) for piano and mixed media where he used a sequencer to randomize the rhythms. The rhythmic complexity resulting from randomization was aesthetically pleasing to Zhou but made the work extremely difficult to perform.

During his conservatory years, Zhou became "obsessed with percussion." As a nod to Varèse, Zhou introduced a battery of percussion instruments, including Western ones, to a Chinese traditional ensemble in *Valley Stream* (1983) and expanded the approach to percussion within the Chinese performance medium in his *Triptych of Bell-Drum Music* for solo percussion (1984). Such a work for solo percussionist was unprecedented in the Chinese musical tradition.

The contrast in Zhou and Chen's transition to America further highlights their personality differences and thus their creativity. Zhou's first two years of struggle in the United States due to culture shock and the loss of his parents inspired a period of introspection and Buddhist meditation that led to his most experimental works (1987–95). During this time, he wanted to "put down his ambitions." Extended techniques that capture the sounds of Chinese instruments remain despite their adventurous dissonance, disjunct textures, and complex rhythmic treatments. Chen recalled that for three years, Zhou took a class on twentieth-century practice, where he learned about extended techniques on Western instruments. This was critical for him in adapting the techniques of Chinese traditional instruments to Western ones. His chamber works, *Soul, Heng, Ding,* and *Dhyana,* are among his most well-known from this period. *Ding* is the only work where he explored twelve-tone techniques, a telling indication of Zhou's convictions, given the dominance of the Second Viennese School at Columbia at that time. Nevertheless, Zhou enjoyed composing *Ding*. It gave him the confidence to compose after two years of struggle. In subsequent works, however, he sought more freedom; sharing in reference to twelve-tone matrices, "With the magic square, you have to follow the numbers." His passion for instrumentation, employing Chinese traditional ensemble techniques, textures, and sonorities in his Western instrumental works, infusing modernist qualities in his traditional ensemble works, or mixing the instrumentation, remained a thread throughout these formative years and continues to the present. It has been a defining aspect of Zhou's cultural synthesis – a holistic contemporary fusion inspired by China's classical past.

Chen's transition to the United States, by contrast, was very smooth. Though in need of greater English proficiency, Chen adjusted quickly and felt "at home" since Cantonese is spoken in New York City's Chinatown. Her outgoing nature is reflected in the wide range of Western techniques she adopted to expand her music's harmonic language, textural variety, and sonic and emotional range before and after her move to America. Varèse's percussion experiments inspired her *Two Sets of Wind and Percussion Instruments* (1986). Bartók's atonality in Concerto for Orchestra and Lutoslawski's aleatoric treatments found expression in Symphony No. 1 (1986). In *As in a Dream* (1987), Chen employed *Sprechstimme*, a treatment that resonated with her perfect pitch translations of Chinese speech. At the conclusion of *Near Distance* (1988), she employed a vocable "SSS" in imitation of electronic music. And, from 1991 onward, a period Chen refers to as her most "academic," she incorporated Goehr's flexible approach to twelve-tone techniques. Works such as *Sparkle* (1992), Piano Concerto (1992), Symphony No. 2 (1993), and *Song in Winter* (1993) fall in this category. Although Chen's experiments with twelve-tone methods began as early as *Duo Ye* (1984) and the Woodwind Quintet (1987), she drew upon this technique more frequently toward the end of her Columbia years, but always in service of the expressed emotions.

Her works from 1984 on also demonstrate a more synthesized compositional practice in their combined use of twelve-tone techniques and Chinese theoretical discoveries. *Duo Ye*, for example, displays palindromic sequences and mathematical patterns of *Shifan luogu* (1, 2, 3, 5, 3, 2, 1) for pitch groupings. With Chou's emphasis on "how philosophy and aesthetics interpret nature" and Davidovsky's encouragement to pursue greater logic and objectivity for structure, Chen used the Golden Mean and the Fibonacci Series from the folk tune *"Baban"* with its eight-beat patterns and three-hundred variations to inform her works: "If I create my music in a language that I am most familiar with, meeting some principles that are related to nature logically, then my creation would be very natural in emotion and powerful in spirit. I think it's ideal" (Borger, 1999, p. 280). Works such as *Sparkle*, Piano Concerto, and *Song in Winter* demonstrate these uses in melody, rhythm, and/or structure. Drawing on such tools as found in nature offered Chen a means for creating a compelling yet transnational expression.

5.3 Conclusion

The study of the external and internal factors that shaped Zhou and Chen's creativity is complex and made more complicated by the fluid way that one's nature and nurture interact. Nevertheless, by examining the external factors that shaped their modernisms, which include family background, early childhood exposures, and reeducation period experiences, notable similarities and differences emerge. The greatest similarity was the extent of musical exposure and tutelage they had prior to entering conservatory, made possible through their supportive and artistically minded families. The most outstanding difference, however, was the nature of their early training from a musical and cultural standpoint. Zhou was not a prodigy at an instrument but possesses a profound musical instinct that was honed through work experiences as a composer for the Zhangjiakou Song and Dance Troupe and the National Broadcasting Symphony Orchestra of China (CNBC). He composes intuitively, inspired by classical Chinese images and text. Chen, on the other hand, was a violin prodigy and spent much of her pre-conservatory days studying and playing Eurocentric violin works, even as concertmaster of Guangzhou's Beijing Opera Troupe. She approaches her compositions structurally with an attention to analyzable details.

Once they arrived at the Central Conservatory and later Columbia University, the differences in their aesthetic preferences and personalities became apparent as they integrated their Chinese cultural identity with the modernist techniques they were learning. Zhou gravitated to Chou's philosophical influence with his explorations of ancient Chinese art forms. The rhythms, meters, language, and textures of Chou, Stravinsky, Respighi, and Varèse among others made their imprint. Zhou's principal area of investigation was cross-cultural instrumentation: (1) Western instruments adopting the style and sounds of *guqin*, percussion, and other Chinese instruments, (2) introducing atonality and modernism to Chinese traditional ensembles, or (3) composing works that combined Western and Chinese instruments. In all these approaches, rhythm, meter, and variety of sonic textures and treatments were his primary emphases.

For Chen, who grew up with Eurocentric musical training, finding an authentic integration of Chinese folk songs and other indigenous expressions in the context of Western formal structures became her focus. Also, expanding her vocabulary of compositional techniques, both Western and Eastern in service of her emotions and desire to connect with the world, was central. She achieved this through the assimilation of atonality, twelve-tone technique, *Baban* proportions, and others.

Perhaps the best way to capture the divergence of their early modernisms is through their descriptions of the creative process. Zhou distinguished his from Chen's as follows:

> Chen Yi usually starts a composition with a map, a secret map on a very small piece of paper. She puts everything on it and follows the map. This is not my style. I compose with maybe just elements or motifs that come to my mind. I will notate them down. So, then I have many ideas and I put it on the paper and put it around me. And I look at all these materials, all these parts, and I assemble everything together. But Chen Yi already has a more logical structure or plan. I still believe in my feelings rather than a plan.

Sometimes she plans very logically the material and the structure, but in the end, I always give her some comments about my feelings. I say, this timing is not enough, or this portion is not enough.

In relationship to setting text or composing instrumental music inspired by poetry, Chen shared:

For some [works], I use a mathematical principle to construct the music. And so, it doesn't mean that this mathematical plan will match the expression [of the text], but I follow the structural plan ... And in Zhou Long's music, he takes it as a whole. The whole piece is dedicated to these whole images. It's abstract. It's not in detail. You can see it as a whole picture, but you can't go into the details.

By the time Zhou and Chen graduated from Columbia, a compelling synthesis of Western modernist techniques and Chinese cultural elements had been achieved in their works. Though their personal narratives bore similarities, their unique natures, and thus their modernisms went separate ways. In Zhou's words, "the music is really attached to your personality. You just can't change it . . . . I believe it's not really easy to change your personality. That's your music, your language."

Glossary of Chinese Traditional Instruments

bangdi: high-register bamboo flute (like a piccolo) from the dizi family

banhu: bowed two-string instrument with a coconut shell body in the huqin family

daruan or ruan: round-bodied lute with four strings and frets

dizi: transverse flute made of bamboo with an additional hole covered by a thin membrane that creates a distinct buzzing quality

erhu: two-string bowed spike fiddle of the huqin family

gaohu: bowed string instrument developed from the erhu but with a smaller soundbox and tuned a fourth higher

guan: double-reed wind instrument made of bamboo

guanzi: northern Chinese version of the guan

guqin or qin: plucked seven-string zither from ancient Chinese culture associated with Confucius and high culture

jing erhu: two-string bowed instrument from the huqin family that is an octave lower in pitch than the *jinghu*

jinghu: small erhu instrument used to accompany Beijing opera

liuqin: multistring mandolin with a pear-shaped body

pipa: pear-shaped lute with frets

qin: see "guqin"

ruan: see "daruan"

sanxian: three-string lute without frets

sheng: mouth-blown free-reed instrument with vertical pipes made of bamboo

xun: round-vessel flute made of stone, clay, or bone with blowing and finger holes

yangqin: hammered dulcimer with seven or more metal strings

yueqin: round-bodied lute with four strings and a short-fretted neck

zheng: plucked zither with twenty-one strings and movable bridges

zhudl: see "dizi"

Lists of Works

ZHOU LONG: LIST OF WORKS

Year	Solo Instrument	Voice	Chamber (Western or Chinese Traditional)	Orchestra	Chorus	Stage
1978	*Song Beneath the Moon* for piano (arr. for two guanzi, yangqin, 1983)					
1979		*Ballade of the Sea* for soprano, piano				
1980	*Mongolian Folk-Tune Variations* for piano					
1981				*Fisherman's Song* for large orchestra		
1982			*Song of the Ch'in* for string quartet		*Words of the Sun* for mixed chorus; revised 1997	

(cont.)

ZHOU LONG: LIST OF WORKS

Year	Solo Instrument	Voice	Chamber (Western or Chinese Traditional)	Orchestra	Chorus	Stage
1983	*Wu Kui* for piano; rev. 2000		*Partita* for violin, piano, rev. 2000 *Taiping Drum* for violin, piano (arr. for erhu, pipa) *Valley Stream* for dizi, guan, zheng, percussion	*Guang Ling San Symphony* for large orchestra		*Dong Shi* (ballet), orchestra
1984	*Triptych of Bell-Drum Music* for percussion		*Green* for bamboo flute, pipa (arr. for soprano, pipa, 1991) *Su* for flute, qin (arr. for flute, harp, pipa, 1990)			
1985						
1986			*The Moon Rising High* for pipa and traditional ensemble (dizi, daruan, yangqin, zheng, erhu, percussion)			

ZHOU LONG: LIST OF WORKS

Year	Solo Instrument	Voice	Chamber (Western or Chinese Traditional)	Orchestra	Chorus	Stage
1987			*Heng* ("Eternity") for dizi, pipa, yangqin, zheng, erhu, percussion, 1987 *Soul* for string quartet (arr. for pipa, string quartet, 1992) *Wu Ji* for piano, fixed media (arr. for zheng, piano, percussion, 1991; piano, percussion, 2000)			
1988		*Li Sao Cantata* for soprano, small orchestra (14 players)	*Ding* ("Samadhi") for clarinet, double bass, percussion (arr. for clarinet, zheng, double bass, 1990)			
1989		*A Poetess' Lament* for soprano, pipa, zheng, erhu; revised 2000	*Variations on A Poetess' Lament* for Chinese instrumental ensemble, fixed media (incidental dance music) *Dunhuang Music* for pipa, zheng, daruan, dizi, sheng, percussion; (*Flying Apsaras of Dunhuang*, electronic dance music version of *Dunhuang Music*, 1986)			*Sheng Sheng Man* (incidental music for dance), soprano, ensemble of Chinese traditional instruments

ZHOU LONG: LIST OF WORKS

Year	Solo Instrument	Voice	Chamber (Western or Chinese Traditional)	Orchestra	Chorus	Stage
1990		*Shi Jing Cantata* for soprano, flute, oboe, clarinet, bassoon, 2 violins, viola, cello, double bass, piano (also version of two sections as *Two Poems* for mixed chorus)	*Han Chinese Folk Songs* for Chinese instrumental ensemble *Dhyana* for flute, clarinet, violin, cello, piano			
1991		*Pipa Ballad* for soprano, pipa, cello	*You Lan* for erhu, piano (arr. as *Secluded Orchid* for violin, cello, piano, 1992; pipa, erhu, cello, percussion, 2000)	*King Chu Doffs His Armor* for pipa, orchestra (arr. for pipa, traditional instruments orchestra) *Da Qu* for Chinese percussion, Hong Kong Chinese traditional orchestra (arr. for percussion, large Western orchestra)		

Year	Solo Instrument	Voice	Chamber (Western or Chinese Traditional)	Orchestra	Chorus	Stage
1992				*Tian Ling* "Nature and Spirit" for pipa, 14 Western instruments (woodwinds, brass, percussion, strings)		
1993	*Wild Grass* for solo cello (arr. for viola)					

CHEN YI: LIST OF WORKS

Year	Solo Instrument	Voice	Chamber (Western or Chinese Traditional)	Orchestra	Chorus
1978					
1979	*Variations on "Awariguli"* for piano		*Fisherman's Song* for violin, piano		
1980					
1981					
1982			**String Quartet** (*Shuo*, arr. of 1st movt. for string orchestra, 1994) *Xian Shi* for viola, piano, percussion		
1983				*Xian Shi,* for viola, orchestra (arr. of trio for viola, piano, percussion, 1982)	

1984	***Duo Ye*** for piano, (arr. for solo pipa, 1995)		
1985	***Yu Diao*** for piano	***Xie Zi*** for liuqin, pipa, sanxian, sheng, bangdi, zhudi, percussion	***Duo Ye No. 1*** for chamber orchestra (arr. of solo piano work)	***Three Poems from the Song Dynasty*** for SATB with divisi up to SSSAAATTBB; SAT solos
1986			***Sprout*** for string orchestra (arr. of 2nd mov't. from String Quartet) ***Symphony No. 1*** for large orchestra ***Two Sets of Wind and Percussion Instruments*** for small orchestra (piccolo, bass clarinet, 15 brass, timpani, 6 percussion)

(cont.)

CHEN YI: LIST OF WORKS

Year	Solo Instrument	Voice	Chamber (Western or Chinese Traditional)	Orchestra	Chorus
1987			Woodwind Quintet No. 1	*Duo Ye No. 2* for orchestra	
1988		*As in a Dream* for soprano, violin, cello (arr. for soprano, pipa, zheng, 1994; soprano, zheng, 2010)	*Near Distance*, sextet for flute, clarinet, violin, cello, piano, percussion *The Tide*, septet for xun, yangqin, pipa, zheng, gaohu, erhu, percussion		
1989	*Guessing* for piano			Overture No. 1 for orchestra of Chinese instruments	
1990				Overture No. 2 for orchestra of Chinese instruments	
1991	*The Points* for pipa		*Suite*, quintet for pipa, dizi, yangqin, sanxian, erhu		

1992		**Sparkle,** octet for flute, clarinet, violin, cello, double bass, two percussionists, piano	**Piano Concerto Pipa Rhyme** for pipa and small orchestra (14 players)
1993	*Monologue – Impressions on the True Story of Ah Q* for clarinet *Small Beijing Gong* for piano	*Song in Winter,* trio for dizi, zheng, and harpsichord (arr. for flute, zheng, piano, percussion, 1993; soprano, zheng, piano, 2004)	**Symphony No. 2**

Bibliography

Arlin, M. I., & Radice, M. A. (2018). *Polycultural Synthesis in the Music of Chou Wen-Chung*, New York: Routledge.

Bonnin, M. (2013). *The Lost Generation: The Rustication of China's Educated Youth (1968–1980)*, Hong Kong: The Chinese University of Hong Kong Press.

Borger, I., ed. (1999). *The Force of Curiosity*, Santa Monica: Calarts.

Cai, J., & Melvin, S. (2004). *Rhapsody in Red: How Western Classical Music Became Chinese*, New York: Algora Publishing.

Chang, P. (2001). Chou Wen-Chung's Cross-Cultural Experience and His Musical Synthesis: The Concept of Syncretism Revisited. *Asian Music*, 32 (2), 93–118, DOI: https://doi.org/10.2307/834250.

Chang, P. (2006). *Chou Wen-Chung: The Life and Work of a Contemporary Chinese-Born American Composer*, Lanham, MD: Scarecrow Press, Inc.

Chen, Y. (1986). Program notes for Symphony No. 1.

Chen, Y. (1993). Piano Concerto, unpublished DMA diss., Columbia University.

Chen, Y. (1993). Program notes for Symphony No. 2.

Chen, Y. (2002). Tradition and Creation. *Current Musicology*, 67/68, 59–72.

Chen, Y., Fan, Z., Gu, X., & Zhou, L. A. (2020). Arrival of Young Talent: The Send-Down Movement and Rural Education in China. *American Economic Review*, 110 (11), 3393–3430, DOI: https://doi:10.1257/aer.20191414.

Chou, W. C. (1966). Open Rather Than Bounded. *Perspectives of New Music*, 5 (1), 1–6.

Chou, W. C. (1968–9). East and West, Old and New. *Asian Music*, 1 (1), 19–22.

Chou, W. C. (1978). A Visit to Modern China. *The World of Music*, 20 (2), 40–44.

Chou, W. C. (2007). Whither Chinese Composers? *Contemporary Music Review*, 26 (5/6), 501–510, DOI: https://doi.org/10.1080/07494460701652939.

Clark, P., Pang, L., & Tsai, T. H., eds. (2016). *Listening to China's Cultural Revolution: Music, Politics, and Cultural Continuities*, London: Palgrave Macmillan.

Da Fonseca-Wollheim, C. (Oct. 29, 2019). Chou Wen-chung, Composer and Calligrapher in Sound, Dies at 96. *New York Times*.

Dai, J. (2016). A Diachronic Study of Jingju Yangbanxi Model Peking Opera Music. In P. Clark, L. Pang, and T. H. Tsai, eds., *Listening to China's Cultural Revolution: Music, Politics, and Cultural Continuities*, London: Palgrave Macmillan, pp. 11–36.

De Bary, T., & Lufrano, R. (2000). *Sources of Chinese Tradition: From 1600 Through the Twentieth Century*, vol. 2, 2nd ed., New York: Columbia University Press.

Edwards, J. M., & Miller, L. (2020). *Chen Yi*, Champaign: University of Illinois Press.

Everett, W. A., & Tibbetts, J. C. (2018). Chen Yi and Zhou Long: "We Strive to Combine the Culture of East and West." In W. A. Everett, M. Saffle, and J. C. Tibbetts, eds., *Musical Multiplicities in the Twentieth and Twenty-First Centuries, Performing Music History*, London: Palgrave Macmillan, pp. 283–288, DOI: https://doi.org/10.1007/978-3-319-92471-7_9.

Green, E. (2007). The Impact of Buddhist Thought on the Music of Zhou Long: A Consideration of Dhyana. *Contemporary Music Review*, 26 (5/6), 547–567, DOI: https://doi.org:10.1080/07494460701652970.

Griffiths, P. (1985). *New Sounds, New Perspectives: British Composers of the 1980s in Conversation with Paul Griffiths*, London: Faber & Faber.

Jiao, W. (2014). *Chinese and Western Elements in Contemporary Chinese Composer Zhou Long's Works for Solo Piano Mongolian Folk-Tune Variations, Wu Kui, and Pianogongs*, unpublished DMA diss., University of North Carolina at Greensboro.

Joseph, W. A., Wong, C. P. W., & Zweig, D., eds. (1991). *New Perspectives on the Cultural Revolution*, Cambridge, MA: Harvard University Council on East Asian Studies.

Kouwenhoven, F. (1992). Developments in Mainland China's New Music, Part 1: From China to the United States. *China Information*, 7 (1), 17–39.

Kouwenhoven, F., & Schimmelpenninck, A. (1993). History & Foreign Students' Experiences: The Shanghai Conservatory of Music. *CHIME*, No. 6, Spring, pp. 56–91.

Kraus, R. C. (2004). *The Party and the Arty in China: The New Politics of Culture*, Lanham, MD: Rowman & Littlefield Publishers, Inc.

Li, J. (2004). *Chinese Musical Structure: An Outline Analysis*, Beijing: Central Conservatory of Music Publishing Company.

Liu, C. (2010). *A Critical History of New Music in China*, Hong Kong: The Chinese University of Hong Kong Press.

Ludden, Y. (2013). *China's Musical Revolution: From Beijing Opera to Yangbanxi*, PhD diss., University of Kentucky. https://uknowledge.uky.edu/music_etds/19/

McDougall, B. (1980). *Talks at the Yan'an Conference on Literature and Art: A Translation of the 1943 Text with Commentary*, Ann Arbor: University of Michigan Center for Chinese Studies.

Mittler, B. (1997). *Dangerous Tunes: The Politics of Chinese Music in Hong Kong, Taiwan, and the People's Republic of China Since 1949*, Wiesbaden: Harrossowitz.

Mittler, B. (2012). *A Continuous Revolution: Making Sense of Cultural Revolution Culture*, Cambridge, MA: Harvard University Asia Center.

Ouyang, L. X. (2022). *Music as Mao's Weapon: Remembering the Cultural Revolution*, Champaign: University of Illinois Press.

Rao, N. (2007). The Tradition of *Luogu Dianzi* (Percussion Classics) and Its Signification in Contemporary Music. *Contemporary Music Review*, 26 (5/6), 511–527, DOI: https://doi.org/10.1080/07494460701652947.

Roche Commissions. (2005). *Chen Yi*, Lucerne: Roche Pharmaceuticals.

Roeder, J. (2020). Interactions of Folk Melody and Transformational (Dis) continuities in Chen Yi's *Ba Ban* (1999). *Music Theory Online*, 26 (3), 1–9, www.mtosmt.org/issues/mto.20.26.3/mto.20.26.3.roeder.php.

Saffle, M., & Yang, H. L., eds. (2017). *China and the West: Music, Representation, and Reception*, Ann Arbor: University of Michigan Press.

Sakakibara, A. (2014). A Longitudinal Study of the Process of Acquiring Absolute Pitch: A Practical Report of Training with the "Chord Identification Method." *Psychology of Music*, 42 (1), 86–111, DOI: https://doi.org/10.1177/0305735612463948.

Saywell, W. G. (1980). Education in China Since Mao. *The Canadian Journal of Higher Education*, Vol. X-1, 1–27, DOI: https://doi.org/10.47678/cjhe.v10i1.182805.

Schonberg, H. (1997). *The Lives of the Great Composers*, 3rd ed., New York: W. W. Norton & Co.

The Economist Explains. (June 23, 2021). How Did Confucianism Win Back the Communist Party? *The Economist*. www.economist.com/the-economist-explains/2021/06/23/how-did-confucianism-win-back-the-chinese-communist-party.

Wong, H. Y. (2007). Bartók's Influence on Chinese New Music in the Post-Cultural Revolution Era. *Studia Musicologica*, 48 (1/2), 237–243, DOI: https://doi.org/10.1556/smus.48.2007.1-2.16.

Zheng, S. (2010). *Claiming Diaspora: Music, Transnationalism, and Cultural Politics in Asian/Chinese America*, New York: Oxford University Press.

Zhou, L. (1993). *Daqu* for percussion and orchestra, unpublished DMA diss., Columbia University.

Zhou, L. (2002). *Wu Kui* for piano, Oxford: Oxford University Press.

Zhou, L. (2005). *Ding* for clarinet, percussion, and double bass, Oxford: Oxford University Press.

Cambridge Elements ≡

Music Since 1945

Mervyn Cooke
University of Nottingham

Mervyn Cooke brings to the role of series editor an unusually broad range of expertise, having published widely in the fields of twentieth-century opera, concert and theatre music, jazz, and film music. He has edited and co-edited *Cambridge Companions to Britten, Jazz, Twentieth-Century Opera*, and *Film Music*. His other books include *Britten: War Requiem, Britten and the Far East, A History of Film Music, The Hollywood Film Music Reader, Pat Metheny: The ECM Years*, and two illustrated histories of jazz. He is currently co-editing (with Christopher R. Wilson) *The Oxford Handbook of Shakespeare and Music*.

About the Series

Elements in Music Since 1945 is a highly stimulating collection of authoritative online essays that reflects the latest research into a wide range of musical topics of international significance since the Second World War. Individual Elements are organised into constantly evolving clusters devoted to such topics as art music, jazz, music and image, stage and screen genres, music and media, music and place, immersive music, music and movement, music and politics, music and conflict, and music and society. The latest research questions in theory, criticism, musicology, composition and performance are also given cutting-edge and thought-provoking coverage. The digital-first format allows authors to respond rapidly to new research trends, with contributions being updated to reflect the latest thinking in their fields, and the essays are enhanced by the provision of an exciting range of online resources.

Cambridge Elements ☰

Music Since 1945

Elements in the Series

A full series listing is available at: www.cambridge.org/em45

Printed in the United States
by Baker & Taylor Publisher Services